Amazing London Walks

By G. Costa

Table of Contents

How to use this book:

1) Use the Table of Contents to choose one of the tour areas that interests you. Alternatively, if you are unfamiliar with the city's layout, see our walk overview map on the contents page which gives you a rough idea of the area that each walk covers.

2) On the first page of the walk you have some basic information about the tour and a map to help you along the route.

3) Follow the steps and enjoy your walk. Each major sight is listed in red and with a number, which corresponds with a number on the map for that walk.

4) If you prefer a digital version of these maps, please visit http://bit.ly/amazingwalks to download high-quality versions of the maps in this guide. On the website, right-click the maps and save them. You can then print these out if you wish.

Walk 1: Mayfair
Walk Length: 4.4 km/2.7 mi
Timings: 1h 30m (fast), 2h (regular), 2h 30m (leisurely)
Start: Hyde Park Corner station
End: Green Park station or Piccadilly Circus station

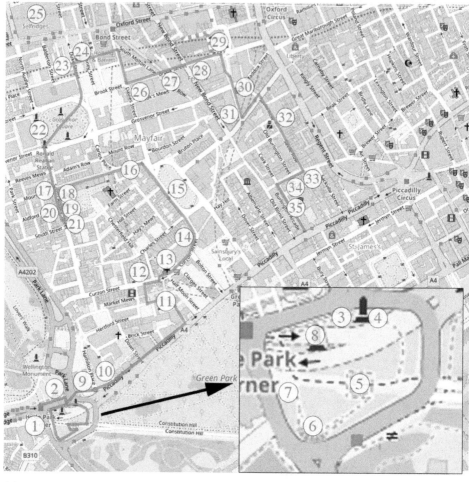

(1) Lanesborough Hotel
(2) Apsley House
(3) Machine Gun Corps Memorial
(4) New Zealand War Memorial
(5) Wellington Arch
(6) Australian War Memorial
(7) Royal Artillery Memorial
(8) Duke of Wellington
(9) Intercontinental Hotel
(10) Hard Rock Cafe
(11) Shepherd Market
(12) Embassy of Saudi Arabia
(13) Third Church of Christ Scientist
(14) The Lansdowne Club
(15) Berkeley Square
(16) Mount Street
(17) James Purdey & Sons
(18) Harry's Bar

(19) The Grosvenor Chapel
(20) Constance Spry Plaque
(21) Thomas Goode & Co.
(22) Grosvenor Square
(23) Electricity Substation
(24) Ukrainian Catholic Church
(25) Selfridges
(26) Claridge's Hotel
(27) Handel and Hendrix Museum
(28) Fenwick
(29) Hanover Square
(30) St. George's Church
(31) Sotheby's
(32) Savile Row
(33) Ede and Ravenscoft
(34) Burlington House
(35) Burlington Arcade

Begin at Hyde Park Corner Station. Use Exit 1 (Hyde Park).

Welcome to Hyde Park Corner – despite the name of the tube station in this area, the street signs tell you that this location is officially called Duke of Wellington Place. Named, after the man whom defeated Napoleon Bonaparte at the Battle of Waterloo in 1815. As you start on the corner here, look over to the opposite side of the road for an opulent white building – this is

the Lanesborough Hotel (1), where one night in the top suite can cost in excess of 30,000 pounds. Breakfast is, naturally, an extra charge. For the price you get to stay in a former hospital, with the current building dating back to 1844 – though a hospital had been on the site over 100 years earlier.

The area going west from here is Knightsbridge, which we will explore later. Instead, we will be venturing east.

Walk in the direction of traffic past the archways and columns with green railings on your left towards the grand yellow-coloured stone house.

This grand house is known as Apsley House (2) and is home to the Duke of Wellington, as well as a museum and art gallery which is open to the public. The house is also known as Number One, London as it was the first building visitors would encounter when they entered the city from the fields of the west – the current building dates from 1771.

Turn the corner on the pavement towards Park Lane and take the subway (the underground passageway – not a train) down underneath this busy intersection. Down the stairs, turn left then take the first right to the centre of the round-about.

Now that you are on the main roundabout, we will take a look at what this area has to offer by making our way round in a clock-wise direction – with the flow of traffic. You will notice a common theme as you make your way around – war and honouring the war-dead.

You will see a statue ahead that may look familiar of a man standing with a sword in his hand. This is The Boy David or the Machine Gun Corps Memorial (3) to WWI. When first unveiled in 1915 in a nearby location, the memorial caused a large amount of controversy because of the perception of this beautiful statue glorifying war, instead of showing its harsh realities. Further ahead, you will see what appears to be spikes rising out of the ground, this is the New Zealand War Memorial (4). Having stood here since 2006, this memorial commemorates those who lost their lives in both World Wars. The 16 bronze girders are intended to represent a group of soldiers marching.

Continue around this large traffic island. You will come to an opening with a pathway leading underneath the glorious Wellington Arch (5). We will come to this shortly, as this is the back of the monument.

Walking past the arch, on the corner, you will see the Australian War Memorial (6). Made of granite slabs from Western Australia, this large memorial when looked at close up lists over 23,000 towns where soldiers came from in Australia. When viewed from a distance, the text from these town names form large words – the 47 battles in which the country fought. In warmer months, the memorial's water system is activated and a small current of water flows on the outer walls.

Next, is the Royal Artillery Memorial (7). This commemorates the Battle of the Somme in 1916 where 55,000 soldiers lost their lives in 1916.

Now following the roundabout you will see our final statue of the Duke of Wellington (8) upon his horse, Copenhagen – standing proud facing the family home in Apsley House.

Turning back, you will see the centrepiece of the roundabout, the Wellington Arch (5) – considerably more impressive than Marble Arch, which is located just up the road on the other end of Park Lane. Designed by Decimus Burton, it dates back to 1826 and was moved to its current location in the 1880s. It now stands at the foot of Constitution Hill and the Queens Life Guard horses pass through the archway daily on their way to and from the Changing of the Horse Guards.

7

Atop the arch, is a statue of Quadriga – a chariot being pulled by four horses. Nike, the Goddess of Victory, descends upon the chariot. This is still the largest bronze sculpture in Europe.

If you fancy something unique to do, head to the archway and you can step foot inside it as it is hollow – here lies an exhibition on the creation of the arch and another of the Battle of Waterloo. You can also climb to the top. The archway is open daily and admission is about 5 pounds.

Now that you have looped the entire roundabout, take the pedestrian subway you used to enter the roundabout, turn left at the bottom of the stairs and then right at the end of the corridor.

5

You emerge by a large white building which today is an Intercontinental Hotel. You are now officially on the corner of London's most prized area – Mayfair. The Intercontinental Park Lane hotel (9) sits on the site of the 1930s childhood home of Queen Elizabeth II. Unfortunately, the building was destroyed by a bomb blast during the Blitz and the currently building leaves no reminder of the history of this area, no even so much as a solitary blue plaque.

Continue past the hotel down Piccadilly; you will soon come to the Hard Rock Café (10).
Although, today these can be found all around the world, there is something a little special about this one – it was the world's first. Founded by two Americans in June 1971, the venue has proved to be a success – the concept was always simple to understand: eat your lunch or dinner and enjoy music, specifically of the hard rock variety. As well as the main restaurant, right next door is the rock shop.

10

As well as the standard Hard Rock logo-emblazoned T-shirts that many visitors collect, the shop holds a surprising secret. Throughout the day (usually at 20 to 30 minute intervals), you can be taken by a member of staff down into The Vault, which Hard Rock proudly professes to be "London's only rock n' roll museum" featuring items such as one of Hendrix's guitars, Beatles memorabilia and even Slash's outfit from November Rain – the cost for the tour: zilch, nada, zero.

Simply ask a member of staff or stand by the sign in the shop for a free tour. The Vault was also once part of Coutts Bank, the royal family's money was once in here.

Piccadilly in itself (the street, not the famous intersection at the other end) has been around for at least 500 years, though it is hard to track how old this road actually is. However, in the 1610s the street was to get its current moniker – Piccadilly is named after the main item of sale here at the time – piccadills. These are big white, frilly collars that were fashionable during the

Elizabethan era – think of Elizabeth I and Shakespeare and chance are you can imagine what a piccadill looked like.

Piccadilly is a bit of a contrast to the rest of Mayfair which has calm streets and a lack of traffic – here our modern-day obsession with personal transportation is clear as cars speed along.

Continue walking down Piccadilly.

Number 128 Piccadilly, the building right after the Rock Shop, is the Royal Air Force Club – this is a military private member's club where the club has been housed since 1919, having moved from Bruton Street (also in Mayfair). The club houses bedrooms, a bar, a pub, a library, a lounge, a dining room, a business centre, a gym and more. It was officially launched by HRH The Duke of York in 1922. The club has been visited by several monarchs including King George V, Queen Mary and Her Majesty Queen Elizabeth II who is a patron today. Membership is available to anyone who holds or has held a position in the Royal Air Force or other associated entities. Membership is relatively affordable starting at £42.50 for Acting Pilot Officers and Reserve Members to £300 for members of the Honourable Company of Air Pilots.

As you will come to discover, the area of Mayfair is filled with private member's clubs. Right next door for example at number 127 is the Cavalry & Guards Club. Mayfair is also dominated by luxury hotels. We have seen the Intercontinental earlier (with a Hilton and Four Seasons just around the corner), and as you walk down Piccadilly you can't fail to notice the garden wall of the Athenaeum Hotel, followed by the Park Lane Hotel.

Continue along Piccadilly, passing the Embassy of Japan at number 101-104 Piccadilly. You will see a small road on your left called White Horse Street. Turn into this lane and the roar of traffic quickly disappears as you stroll into the very heart of Mayfair.

Be aware that traffic will be running towards you and that the pavements are very narrow here. A parade of shops will soon become visible including a cobbler, a café and even a cigar merchant. This is the side of Mayfair which is not too often show on TV or in guidebooks – a relatively working-class side, unlike most of the area's incredible wealth. You emerge into an opening of roads – this is Shepherd Market (11).

11

Depending on the time of the day you visit, you may either encounter office workers, the social bourgeois or (very occasionally) another visitor or tourist who has left the beaten path every so slightly.

Shepherd Market is key to Mayfair – it is where the whole area developed. It was on this site that a yearly fair took place when this was the countryside – the two-week fair, occurring every May, soon gave the area of Mayfair its current name. The fair was established in the 1660s by King James II and its main purpose was for cattle trading, but it soon became popular with visitors of all social classes.

By the eighteenth century, the yearly fair had been all but killed off as the area had gone through gentrification and several grand houses had been constructed on the land. Edward Shepherd, a local architect, was tasked with developing the site and Shepherd Market was born – this was a parade of shops, with a theatre, a pond and paved roads. The area was complete in 1746, after 11 years of development.

By the 1920s, Shepherd Market was the centre of London's social elite. Today it would be fair to say that the pomp that once surrounded this area has migrated to the more residential streets of Mayfair - while the area still has a certain exclusive feel about it, the mix of eateries and shops for all budgets means that it is certainly a world away from the designer shopping streets of Old Bond Street or St. James's, where you'd struggle to find anything for less than £150.

The village-like feel is still there, however, and it is often easy to forget you are in a city with almost 9 million residents as you walk around these quaint streets. The cafes and restaurants with their outdoor tables spilling out onto the street give the area a somewhat continental vibe, the newsagents inspire hope that Mayfair still has residents around and the art galleries remind you that you are very much still in an area that the social elite live and play.

Walk down Shepherd's Street, taking a right down Trebeck Street to arrive on Curzon Street, facing a large palatial building.

Whilst this street is filled with buildings of all architectural styles, it is the large white house that immediately stands out in front of you. Set back from the main road and detached from the other buildings is Crewe House; this majestic edifice is today the Embassy of Saudi Arabia (12). Crewe House was constructed and designed in 1730 by none other than Edward Shepherd himself, making this one of the last surviving original buildings in Mayfair. Curzon Street is today known for its hedge funds.

12

Turn right and walk along Curzon Street until you reach number 7 across the street.

This building stands out amongst all the others and is home to the Third Church of Christ Scientist (13), a Christian denomination with approximately 85,000 followers. The façade you see dates from 1911. After a large redevelopment was agreed in 1984, the mews at the back of the church was redeveloped into offices and flats and it really is quite something to step foot through a historic looking entrance and see a modern world behind it – the church still holds services to this day on the first floor. Step through the main door if the opportunity arises to see this hidden world you would never imagine from the front.

Now take a look at the two buildings to the left of this church entrance – you will have just walked past them, G. Heywood Hill Ltd which was established in 1936. Nancy Mitford, a novelist and biographer worked here.

Immediately next door is gentlemen's favourite G. F. Trumper at number 9 – a barbers and perfumers. Stepping inside reveals a different world from 21st century London. Classic haircuts, beard trims and shaving are all offered, as well as manicures, pedicures and massages. The shop was established in the late 19th century and the interior still retains the original 20th century glass cabinets and mahogany cubicles.

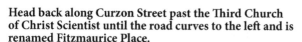

Head back along Curzon Street past the Third Church of Christ Scientist until the road curves to the left and is renamed Fitzmaurice Place.

The large building on your left that dominates half of this street is The Lansdowne Club (14), another of the area's private members' clubs. Lansdowne House, the building, dates back to 1763 and was the first house built on this site, just off Berkeley Square for John Stuart, 3rd Earl of Bute.

The building has been home to several important events in London and England's history: between 1834 and 1852, when the Houses of Parliament were being rebuilt after a fire, the Lansdowne Dining Room was used for meetings of the Privy Council (advisers to the monarch); during WWI, the building was used as a first aid station and 1921, Harry Gordon Selfridge, the American who started one of London's most famous department stores, rented the house from the fifth Marquess of Lansdowne. By 1935, this private residence was now a private members club, with parts of the old house shipped to America.

14

Continue past the Lansdowne Club towards the pedestrian crossings; the street opens out to reveal the first large green space of our walk through Mayfair – **Berkeley Square (15)**.

Berkeley Square is the area of Mayfair that is most associated with business with the vast majority of the buildings being home to hedge funds and wealth management enterprises. The square dates back to the mid-1700s, having been designed by architect William Kent. Unlike many square in areas such as Belgravia and Notting Hill, which are exclusive to residents, this one is open to the public – and indeed the public do use it; note the number of benches in the park which are filled at lunchtime with workers having lunch or on a cigarette break. The London Plane trees on Berkeley Square are amongst the oldest in London, having been planted in 1789.

15

The buildings on the square have been known to a host of historic figures: number 50 is where George Canning lived, politician and four-month-long Prime Minister; number 48 was the childhood home of none other than Winston Churchill; and Charles Rolls, co-founder of Rolls-Royce was born at number 35. The square is today a mix of modern office blocks and Victorian/Georgian Houses.

Keep walking along Berkley Square north towards Porsche, turning left onto Mount Street (16).

In stark contrast to everything you have seen so far, Mount Street has a certain uniformity about it with its terracotta buildings filled with luxury boutiques. This was not always the case, however, for in the 1700s this was far from a quiet luxury retreat – Mount Street was a main thoroughfare to and from the gallows at Tyburn. In the mid-1800s, the Grosvenor family had it modified to its current state.

It would be impossible to visit Mayfair without touching on the Grosvenor family and the Grosvenor estate. This family and their company owns vast swathes of land in London

16

including a large part of Mayfair, as well as Belgravia and have assets worth approximately $60 billion as of 2016. The story goes back to 1677 when Sir Thomas Grosvenor married Mary Davies, who had inherited the manor of Ebury, including 500 acres of swamp, pasture and orchards to the west of London. The Grosvenor family slowly began developing approximately 100 acres of this vast estate in the 1720s – that area is Mayfair today.

Continue to stroll down Mount Street.

Chances are you will not find many people in this area of town unless you are here in the evening when Scott's Restaurant on the right (renowned for its fish) and The Audley pub bring the place to live. This is undoubtedly one of the most exclusive areas of the city.

When you reach the end of the road, South Audley Street runs perpendicular. On the left at the junction of the two streets at the level of the first floor is an old street sign for Mount Street dating back to 1893, followed by a faded street sign painted onto the wall to the right of it and

then the modern standardised street signs by the City of Westminster beneath it. How times change.

Just across on the other side, you will see a large crest above a doorway for James Purdey & Sons (17). Purdey & Sons is the kind of shop that could only seemingly exist in a community such as Mayfair – with three royal warrants from the H.R.H. Duke of Edinburgh, Her Majesty Queen Elizabeth II and

H.R.H. The Duke of Edinburgh you would be hard pressed to find a finer place for guns and rifles, expertly crafted since 1814.

Brief detour – Turn left (south) down South Audley Street. Just ahead, on the left at number 26 is one of the most sophisticated private member's clubs – Harry's Bar (18).

At Harry's Bar the use of mobile phones is not allowed, £1000 a week is spent on flowers for decoration, and alumni include Beyoncé and David Walliams. Inside you will find Venetian chandeliers, Fortuny fabrics and Murano glassware. The annual membership charge is believed to be £1500, plus a £500 inscription fee, and you must be referred by another member. A 3-course meal here, without wine, will usually set members back an eye-watering £170-£200 per person.

Immediately ahead is The Grosvenor Chapel (19), a Church of England church.

The church dates back to 1730 when the foundation stone was laid by Sir Richard Grosvenor, owner of the surrounding property. The building was completed in April 1731. The font inside dates from 1841. The church is most significantly remembered as the location where American troops were welcomed for Sunday services during WWII (a plaque in a bricked up window to the left of the main entrance remembers this). After the War the congregation regularly included such people as the writer Rose Macaulay and Sir John Betjeman, Poet Laureate from 1972 until his death in 1984.

Across the street at number 65, look out for a blue plaque at street level.

This was where a florist called Constance Spry (20) opened her flagship shop in 1934. She was known as "the most fashionable florist in London". Spry published 13 books and even established a school teaching flower arranging techniques. Spry was unconventional refusing to limit herself to the standard flowers in arrangements which were used during the past Victorian and Edwardian eras such as "carnations and asparagus fern", and used wild flowers, twigs, moss, vegetables and anything else that came to mind to spruce up her decorations. She wasn't just arranging flowers, she was decorating with them.

Spry's unconventional methods including buying unusual vases from junk shops and insisting that decorations were composed 'in situ' where they would be displayed and not in beforehand in her shop.

She was most notably responsible for overseeing the floral decorations for Queen Elizabeth II's coronation in 1953 including the entire ceremonial route from Buckingham Palace to Westminster Abbey and the church itself. She used flowers from all throughout The Commonwealth as a special request by the Royal Family.

Next up on the left after the church is Thomas Goode & Co (21), which has been trading since 1827 - before Queen Victoria was even the monarch.

Today it holds two Royal Warrants, which signify that the brand supplies to the Royal Household. In this case these were issued by Queen Elizabeth II and Price Charles, Prince of Wales. The shop bills itself as "the home of the world's finest tableware, china and silverware".

The showroom is simply stunning as you can see via a bit of window shopping (or step inside if it is open). There is a focus on British suppliers and craftsmanship, although many items do come from around the world. Be sure to look out for the beautiful twin elephants in the showroom, which have stood sentinel over South Audley Street since Victorian times. Most recently, in 2015, one was lent as the centrepiece of the 'Sculpture Victorious' exhibition at Tate Britain, showing how prized these magnificent statues are.

Go back on yourself up South Audley Street, passing Mount Street on the right as you go.

After passing Purdey & Sons once again, Massimo de Carlo appears shortly on the left, an Italian art dealer with other galleries in Milan and Hong Kong.

Sharing the same building, at number 55, is Mansour on the 2nd floor. Note the Prince of Wales' Royal Warrant above the door. Mansour specialises in antique carpets and tapestries with collections from Europe, Persia and the Orient – many have been part of royalty's homes across the globe. Mansour represents the largest antique rug collection in the world. They sell their craft well: "There is a room in every home for a Mansour rug, and there is a Mansour rug for a room in any home. We know that every piece has a story and, because of its timeless beauty and value, will become a legacy to future generations."

Continue up South Audley Street passing a small high street with estate agents, galleries, restaurants. You soon reach Grosvenor Square (22) and "Little America". Use the crossing to reach the park in the centre.

The large dominating building on the left in the former Embassy of the United States of America. Constructed in the late 1950s, the US moved its embassy here in 1960 from 1 Grosvenor Square. The bald eagle across the top front has a wingspan of 35 feet. Security significantly increased after the 2001 terrorist attacks in New York when the road in front of the embassy was blocked off.

22

The US vacated the embassy in January 2018 and moved to new premises in Nine Elms. The embassy building is now owned by Qatari real-estate investment firm Qatari Dia, who will convert the grade II listed building into a hotel.

Grosvenor Square has a history of American links since the 1780s including having been the home of John Adams at number 9, first American Minister to Great Britain (and later 2nd US President), housed the headquarters of General Dwight D. Eisenhower and the European headquarters of the United States Navy.

In and around the gardens you will find statues to former US presidents Reagan, Eisenhower and Roosevelt, as well as the Eagle Squadrons Memorial remembering the 244 American and 16 British fighter pilots who were part of the three Royal Air Force Eagle Squadrons from 1940 to 1942. There is also the small but peaceful 11 September 2001 Memorial Gardens with the sobering inscription "Grief is the price we pay for love".

The development of Grosvenor Square commenced in 1721 by Sir Robert Grosvenor and it became London's most fashionable address, home to aristocracy until WWII. It is the second largest square in London (the largest being Lincoln Inn's Fields in the law district) It is the roughly in the centre of Mayfair and therefore the estate's focal point. Only number 9 and number 38 survive from the 1700s. Originally all the ground houses would have been surrounded by mews.

Once you have explored the square, exit via the North East corner down Duke Street.

Further along Duke Street on the left, opposite the redbrick church is an unusual structure with large green doors that many may assume is a small temple.

Completed in 1905 by Charles Stanley Peach in a Baroque style, this is actual an elaborate cover for an electricity substation (23) which is underneath. As the substation replaced a garden, the Duke of Westminster insisted that a garden be added on top. If the gates are open, head up the steps to Brown Hart Gardens and see the peaceful paved garden that stands there today.

There was a large refurbishment in 2007 and again in 2012 and there is now a small café.

On the other side of the road is the beautiful red-brick Ukrainian Catholic Church of the Holy Family in Exile (24).

The building the church occupies was designed by Alfred Waterhouse in 1891 for occupation by the Congregational King's Weigh House Chapel. The chapel's name comes from its original foundation as a dissenters' chapel, above the office for checking the weight of merchandise. The building on the present site was funded by a generous gift from the Duke of Westminster. The building was sold to the Ukrainian Catholics in 1967.

23

Cross over to the corner of Weighhouse Street and Duke Street and look down Duke Street towards Oxford Street.

In the distance you should be able to see a building with a yellow flag on the corner. This is the world-renowned Selfridges (25), a department store.

Feel free to go and take a closer look, though you will need to come back to the corner of the Ukrainian Church to continue the tour.

Selfridges is the second largest store in the UK (coming in at 500,000 square feet – around half the size of Harrods). The store was founded in 1908 by an American, Harry Gordon Selfridge. Very few department stores existed in the country at the start of the 20th century and Selfridge sought to encourage people into the idea that shopping could be a leisure activity and not just a necessity. It is said he also came up with the phrase "the customer is always right." Selfridge came up with many ways to entice shoppers including showcasing the latest technology in-store – for example, in 1909 after Louis Bleriot made the first plane crossing of the English channel, he showed off the monoplane in store.

The store was even important during WWII when the basement housed the SIGSALY scrambler which encoded conversations between President Roosevelt in the US and Britain's Winston Churchill so they could no be intercepted.

If you are visiting in November or December it is worth going up close to the store to see the beautiful Christmas window displays. The roof garden, when open, is also worth a visit and if you plan on buying luxury brands, here you have it all under one roof.

Head down Weighhouse Street to the right of the Ukrainian Church.

Note the beautiful stained glass windows of the church, which are an example of the Arts and Crafts Movement. This movement, which eventually spread to mainland Europe and North America, ran from the early 1800s to the 1920s and was a move away from factory-based, mass-produced industrialised processes to handmade, skilled craftsmanship.

As you move down the street on the right hand side of the road look out for the old signs to United Dairies, a now defunct milk distribution company. If you fancy a stop, we recommend "Comptoir Mayfair" (Open Mon to Sat) just after the former home of United Dairies – a great independent coffee shop, restaurant and wine shop fusion concept. This a good stop for a light bite or a full blown meal.

This area is currently undergoing construction for the new Elizabeth Line opening in December 2018, so walking routes may be temporarily closed. This site will in the future hold an entrance to Bond Street station.

Continue along Weighhouse Street and turn right onto Davies Street and turn left onto Brook Street.

The huge, beautiful Victorian red-brick building with the flags outside is Claridge's Hotel (26), which as famous as The Ritz in London. In the early 1800s, Number 51 brook Street was home to a small hotel run by William and Marianne Claridge from a single house. In an ambitious move to expand their business significantly, the couple bought the five adjoining buildings in 1854 to create an enormous hotel. Claridge's opened in its own right in 1856.

26

Claridge's has been a favourite of royalty well before London's Ritz was even around – in 1860, Queen Victoria and Prince Albert visited after hearing of its reputation, in the 1940s it was a refuge for many exiled heads of state during WWII such as the Kings of Greece, Norway and Yugoslavia. It has often been called an "annexe to Buckingham Palace".

More recently, Kate Moss celebrated her 30th birthday at Claridge's. Jade Jagger and Lulu Guinness described the hotel as their ultimate treat and Alex James said Claridge's was just "perfect". Claridge's always has an excellent set of Christmas decorations in its lobby and its tree is often styled by a notable designer. Finally, Claridge's offers one of the highest rated afternoon teas in London in exquisite surroundings.

Take a left down Brook Street and follow the road.

Brook Street, developed in the early 18th century, is named after the Tyburn Brook which ran nearby. Further along the street, at number 23 and 25 on the right hand side, flanked by shops on the ground floor, you will see two blue heritage plaques by the windows on the first floor.

Composer George Frederick Handel lived at number 25 Brook Street from 1723 until his death in 1759. Almost all his works after 1723 were composed and rehearsed here. Next door at number 23 was where rock guitarist Jimi Hendrix lived in 1968-69. Today both these houses are accessible to the public as a museum (entitled "Handel and Hendrix in London" [27]), which greatly expanded in 2016 with the addition of the Hendrix apartment. The museum entrance can be reached by taking the small alley after the Hendrix house on the right (Lancashire Court) and then another right to reach the back of the building (Open Mon to Sat 11:00 to 18:00 - £10 per adult, £5 per child).

Continue ahead on Brook Street crossing over New Bond Street to find the beautiful Fenwick (28) **building on the corner.**

You will no doubt have noticed the number of luxury shops intensify as you walk down Brook Street and, right now, you are at the epicentre of luxury shopping in London – New Bond Street. Bond Street name originates from the street being built on fields surrounding Clarendon House on Piccadilly, which were developed by Sir Thomas Bond – the head of a syndicate of developers. Along the street you will find luxury

28

brands such as Chanel, Tiffany's and many more. We will explore this street further later on in the tour.

Fenwick is a chain of department stores whose roots date back to 1882 when the first store was founded in Newcastle-upon-Tyne by John James Fenwick. The chain first opened its London store on New Bond Street in 1891, and it expanded and doubled in size in 1980. Fenwick is famed for its luxury goods and its window displays, particularly at Christmas.

Continue down Brook Street passing Fenwick.

You will soon reach Hanover Square (29). Until December 2018, there will likely be a lot of work here due to the construction of the Elizabeth Line. This will be the other entrance to Bond Street station, giving you an idea of the immensity of each of the new stations and the length of the trains.

As you reach Hanover Square, it is clear that you have left behind the residential side of Mayfair and are now in the area's prime business district with offices in every direction.

In the centre of the square is a statue of William Pitt the Younger who was Prime Minister between 1804 and 1806 – the time of the French Revolution and the Napoleonic Wars, including during Britain's victory at the Battle of Waterloo.

The square itself was developed starting in 1713 by Richard Lumley, 1st Earl of Scarbrough as a fashionable address. The square's name was a tribute to the House of Hanover which Lumley was such a proud supporter of. In 1714, upon the death of Queen Anne, George I became King ushering in the House of Hanover and the beginning of the 116-year Georgian era in which there were four successive King George's – George I to George IV.

You can see some great example of Georgian buildings which still survive (they are few and far between on this square) at number 16, 20, 21, though the interiors have been heavily upgraded.

Exit the square by going south down St. George Street and soon on the left is St. George's Church (30).

St George's Church was built in the early 1700s and was designed by John James, a contemporary and colleague of famed architect Christopher Wren (in fact James was master carpenter on Wren's beautiful St. Paul's Cathedral). The tower of the church with its coupled columns set diagonally at angles is inspired by Wren's works. The church was part of an ambitious plan in 1710 to build 50 churches to meet London's expanding population – in the end only 12 were built from scratch, and a further 5 were partially rebuilt. St George's still towers everything in the immediate area.

30

Further down the street past the church on the left, housed in a Georgian building, is Shapero Rare Books.

Compared to mostly everything in Mayfair, Shapero is a new arrival on the scene having been founded in 1979, but it has nonetheless cemented its place in Mayfair's history. The shop was described in 2005 by online magazine Slate as "London's most successful rare-book dealer and arguably the top dealer in the world today". The business moved to its current building in 1996.

Across the street is the more recognisable name of Sotheby's (31), the oldest and largest internationally recognised firm of fine art auctioneers in the world.

Founded in 1744 on Strand (near Trafalgar Square today) by Samuel Baker, the company moved to its current location on New Bond Street in 1917 – this is the back of the building.

For more than a century, Baker and his successors focused on books and handled great libraries sold at auction, including those of the Earls of Sunderland, Hopetoun and Pembroke and the Dukes of Devonshire, York and Buckingham. With the move to Mayfair, the company moved from the book world to the art world

31

nd today sells a wide range of fine arts, not restricting itself to one sector.

he building is open to the public outside of auction times too, with galleries displaying items rhich will go on sale in the future. There is also a delightful café which even serves afternoon ea. The auctions are also free, though you must pre-register for a paddle to bid.

ontinue down the road to the junction with Conduit Street and take a left.

hortly on the left you will come across a black shop with gold writing – Rigby and Peller – ome to a Royal Warrant as corsetiere (supplier of undergarments) to Queen Elizabeth II. ounded in 1939, the brand was also used by the late Queen Mother.

ross the street and take the first turning right into Savile Row (32).

riginally named Savile Street, it was built between 1731 and 1735 as part of the development f the Burlington Estate. Today Savile Row is synonymous with tailoring and gentlemen's attire. ailors started doing business on the Burlington Estate in the late 18th century; initially in ork Street, then by 1803 in Savile Row itself.

he term "bespoke" as applied to fine tailoring is thought to have originated in Savile Row, neaning a suit cut and made by hand. A tailor made suit along the street starts at about £3000, vith the average cost being closer to £5000. The typical suit takes 6 months to produce and equires at least two (but sometimes up to four) fittings.

his first section of Savile Row, today looks very modern with glass-fronted buildings. Some f the buildings which stood on this side of the street were destroyed during The Blitz in 1940 - even then, those buildings were only a few years old as the street had only recently been xtended to Connaught Street in the 1930s.

ollow the street and about half way along you will lotice a stepchange in building styles as you reach the lder section of Savile Row.

32

t number 19 is Maurice Sedwell, a relative newcomer o the street having arrived in 1994, though the brand nitially ran from Fleet Street since 1938. In 2008, Anlrew Ramroop, the company owner started the Saville Row Academy in an effort to keep this longstanding radition alive and to expand the industry to be more nclusive – a male-dominated field, the Savile Row Academy's intake today is often close to a 50/50 split between male and female students.

A few doors down at number 15 is Henry Poole and Co., which has been trading since 1806. In .860, one of the most recognised parts of men's eveningwear was created. In this year, Hen-y Poole made a short evening or smoking jacket for the Prince of Wales to wear at informal linner parties at Sandringham.

The story goes that in 1886, James Potter of Tuxedo Park, New York, visited London and was nvited to spend a weekend at Sandringham House by the Prince. To fit in with his surround-ngs, he had a smoking jacket tailor made by the Prince's tailors, Henry Poole & Co. On return-ng to New York, Mr. Potter proudly wore his jacket at the Tuxedo Club and fellow members soon started having others made for themselves; they adopted the jacket as their dinner attire. As a result, the dinner jacket became known as a tuxedo or tux in America.

Further along is Hardy Amies, founded by Sir Edwin Hardy Amies, and has been trading since 1946. Amies was best known for his official title as dressmaker for Queen Elizabeth II, from her accession to the throne 1952 until his retirement in 1989. He established the monarch's crisp, understated style of dress.

As you walk along the street, do keep your eyes peeled: if you look down into the basement of the older buildings you often can see the tailors at work.

Further along, number 3 on the left was the former home of Apple Corps Ltd, including Apple Records – founded by the members of the Beatles in 1968. The Apple Studio was located in the basement, where the Beatles recorded and filmed portions of their album Let It Be.

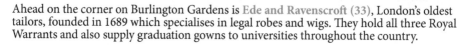

The company was established as a way to reduce the band members' tax liabilities. On the company's founding, John Lennon said: "Our accountant came up and said 'We got this amount of money. Do you want to give it to the government or do something with it?' So we decided to play businessmen for a bit because we've got to run our own affairs now. So we've got this thing called 'Apple' which is going to be records, films, and electronics – which all tie up".

33

Ahead on the corner on Burlington Gardens is Ede and Ravenscroft (33), London's oldest tailors, founded in 1689 which specialises in legal robes and wigs. They hold all three Royal Warrants and also supply graduation gowns to universities throughout the country.

Turn right at this junction onto Burlington Gardens.

Immediately after Ede and Ravenscroft is the back entrance to the Royal Academy of Arts inside the Palladian-style Burlington House (34), named after Richard Boyle, 1st Earl of Burlington, who bought it while it was being built. It was the largest building on the Burlington Estate when it was built in 1664. It was continually altered and expanded until the 1870s.

Since 1854, the building has been owned by the British government, who had originally planned to replace it with a university. After widespread opposition, the building was kept and the site now houses the Royal Academy of arts. Additional side wings today contain the Geological Society of London, Linnean Society of London, Royal Astronomical Society, Society of Antiquaries of London and the Royal Society of Chemistry.

The Royal Academy of Arts contains a paid admission art gallery with continually rotating exhibits. The summer exhibition is the world's largest and longest running open submission show, making it extremely eclectic and garnering submissions from across the globe.

Continue past Burlington House. Take a left through the covered Burlington Arcade (35).

Arcades are indoor shopping areas, originally created to shelter shoppers from the inclement weather – the more expensive shops with the higher profit margins were inside these arcades.

However, the initial arcade's purpose was not solely to create money. In fact, Lord George Cavendish who had inherited Burlington House next door was so annoyed at passers by throwing rubbish over the walls into his gardens that he had the Burlington Arcade built to prevent this. The arcade opened in 1819 and today houses forty small shop units.

Walk through Burlington Arcade.

As you come out of the arcade, be sure to take a look back at the arcade and notice the façade added in the early 1900s in the Victorian Mannerism style of architecture inspired by Italian designs from the 1500s. You may also wish to turn left and see the beautiful façade of Burlington House and enter the courtyard here.

You are now in busy central London on Piccadilly. This is where our walk concludes. From here it is a 4-minute walk to the right for Green Park station or 5-minute walk to the left to Piccadilly Circus station.

35

Walk 2: Royal London: Piccadilly and St. James's

Walk Length: 4.24 km / 2.63 mi
Timings: 2h (fast), 2h 30m (regular), 3h (leisurely)
Start: Green Park station
End: Green Park station

(1) The Ritz	(14) The Naval and Military Club	(26) Carlton House - The Royal Society
(2) White's Club	(15) London Library	(27) Queen Mother & George V Memorial
(3) Brook's	(16) East India Club	(28) Marlborough House
(4) Boodle's	(17) Christie's	(29) Clarence House
(5) Blue Ball Yard	(18) Fortnum and Mason	(30) Lancaster House
(6) John Lobb Bootmaker	(19) Hatchard	(31) Buckingham Palace
(7) Lock and Co.	(20) BAFTA	(32) Victoria Memorial
(8) Pickering Place	(21) St. James's Church	(33) Canada Gates
(9) Berry Bros and Rudd	(22) Black Lamppost	(34) Canada War Memorial
(10) St. James's Palace	(23) The Guards Crimean War Memorial	(35) Green Park
(11) Oxford & Cambridge Club	(24) The Athenaeum	(36) Spencer House
(12) Home of Nell Gywn	(25) Duke of York Column	(37) Diana Fountain
(13) Norfolk House		

Begin at Green Park Station (Exit: Piccadilly Southside)

Welcome to Piccadilly, one of London's busiest main thoroughfares. Piccadilly in itself (the street, not the famous intersection at the other end) has been around for at least 500 years, though it is hard to track how old this road actually is. However, in the 1610s the street was to get its current moniker – Piccadilly is named after the main item of sale here at the time – piccadills. These are big white, frilly collars that were fashionable during the Elizabethan era – think of Elizabeth I and Shakespeare to imagine what a piccadill looked like.

Piccadilly was also at one point called "Portugal Street" after Charles II's Portuguese wife Catherine de Bragança. We will return to the story of Charles II later in the tour.

Perhaps the first thing you will notice on this walk is the imposing sign of The Ritz (1). The Ritz was founded in 1906 by Cezar Ritz who had previously been the manager of the famed The Savoy Hotel and had made the establishment a success. He set up his own venture with the aim of creating the finest hotel in the world. The building's architecture has French influences, being in a Louis XVI neoclassic style, and was designed to resemble a Parisian block of flats (apartments), over covered arcades imitating those of Rue de Rivoli. Ritz wanted his London hotel to innovate and little details such as heated towel bars and a fireplace in every room

attracted nobility to stay. The Ritz is not part of the Ritz-Carlton chain of hotels.

Many famous people have met and/or stayed at the hotel over the years: Dwight Eisenhower and Charles de Gaulle met to discuss operations during WW II; it was the favourite haunt of Charlie Chaplin; playwright Nöel Coward wrote songs at The Ritz; Queen Elizabeth The Queen Mother regularly dined at The Ritz; Sir Roger Moore stayed at the Ritz when he was knighted in 2003; HM Queen Elizabeth II held her 80th birthday celebrations in 2006; and former Prime Minister Margaret Thatcher chose to spend the last nights of her life here as well.

The Ritz now holds a Royal Warrant (a document that confirms the establishment provides goods or services to the royal family, usually accompanied by a crest symbol or royal arms) for banqueting and catering services and its Palm Court is likely the most famous location in the country for afternoon tea – after all, there's nothing quite like saying you are "Going for Tea at The Ritz". The Ritz Club is a casino in the basement of the hotel.

Walk through the covered arcade under The Ritz. Cross the road ahead and continue along Piccadilly, passing The Wolseley on your right (once a car showroom, now an expensive restaurant). Take a right along St. James's Street.

At the end of the street you may make out an imposing building, this is St James's Palace which we will see later on in the tour.

On the opposite side of St James' Street is White's Club (2), the first gentlemen's clubs in London and one of the most exclusive in the world. Gentlemen's clubs began life in the 18th century as private clubs for men to socialise; discussion of trade or business is usually not allowed in gentlemen's clubs.

White's Club was founded in 1693 by an Italian immigrant named Francesco Bianco – curiously it began life as a hot chocolate emporium before becoming a gentlemen's club. White's moved to its current Victorian Palladian-façade building in 1778. To this day, the club does not allow women to become members, or even

enter the premises. Notable current members include Prince Charles and Prince William.

Exceptionally, despite being a lady, Queen Elizabeth II was allowed to visit the club on two occasions – most recently in 2016. The waiting list to become a member runs into several years. Former prime minister David Cameron was a member of White's, but reportedly ended his own membership due to the club's policy of not admitting women.

Continue down St. James's Street.

Further along the road, on the right hand side there is a beautiful imposing building of Brook's (3), another gentlemen's club, which has history dating back to 1764. The clubhouse was built of yellow brick and Portland stone in a Palladian style.

Further along the street is Justerini and Brooks, founded in 1749, and holders of a Royal Warrant for fine wines – they have held this Royal Warrant continually since it was issued by George III in 1761. They also provide wine investing services and hold close to two hundred million pounds of wine on behalf of their customers.

Slightly further across the road at number 28 is Boodle's (4) with the dark bricks, which has strong links to Brook's as the two were originally one club, created as its founder had been rejected from White's.

Continue down St. James's Street, turn right down the next small road into Blue Ball Yard (5) or use the pedestrian entrance. This is easy to miss.

Blue Ball Yard is quite unlike any other place in St. James's and a real hidden gem. This small street, which has been around since at least 1672 when the site was sold by King Charles II, used to be a mews and housed the stables for the houses around it (as well as the area's servants) – back then, it was called Stable Yard.

The street likely changed its name to honour the pub which stood at one end called the "Blue Ball Tavern", demolished in the 18th century. A blue ball sign was often used on buildings at the time to denote a tradesman and, sometimes, a fortune teller.

Today, Blue Ball Yard is an oasis of calm and the buildings here wouldn't look out of place in a small country village. This is in fact the back entrance of the Stafford Hotel. There is also a bar here called 'The American', as the hotel served as accommodation for US and Canadian servicemen during WWII, and the wine cellars below were also used as an air-raid shelter.

Another item of note can be found here in the entrance passageway - the gas lamp. These are often completely missed by most visitors, but there are in fact around 1,500 of these Victorian lamps left in central London, with the largest concentration around the Royal Palaces and Parks, and in Covent Garden.

Originally, these gas lamps would have to be manually lit but today an electric spark is used to light the lamp – a timer, which has to be regulated every 2 weeks to keep up with the seasons, ensures they are only switched on when dusk falls (or at least that's the theory – you will see many of them are switched on during the day). During State Visits, gas lamps near Buckingham Palace are left lit up all day by tradition. British Gas has a specialist team of five men who are responsible for the maintenance of these lamps today.

Head back out onto St James's Street, immediately on the opposite side of the road is James J Fox, the oldest cigar merchant in the world dating back to 1787. Cross over if you want to take a closer look.

Otherwise, turn right and continue along the road and take the pedestrian crossing to the other side. Continue along the street until you reach John Lobb Bootmaker (6).

6

John Lobb was born in 1829 in Cornwall and worked as an apprentice bootmaker in London. Following a successful period in Australia making boots for the miners of the gold rush, he returned to London to set up his first shop on Regent Street in 1866. Lobb quickly established himself as the premier boot and shoemaker of the day, providing a bespoke service to aristocracy, as well as the political and business elite.

Today, at this location, John Lobb Ltd still create custom-made shoes. Each shoe goes through a 190-step creation process, with the shoes on the lower end retailing for £1000 for bath slippers, and reaching in excess of £14,500 for crocodile boots. The shop holds two Royal Warrants: one from Prince Charles, another from Prince Philip.

Almost immediately next door at number 6 is Lock and Co. (7) – the world's oldest hat shop, again with Royal Warrants from Prince Charles and Prince Philip.

7

The company was founded in 1676 and the shop has been in its current location since 1765. Lock and Co were the creators of the bowler hat – designed as the perfect hat for gamekeepers: top hats were too fragile and too tall.

Notable shoppers here have included Beau Brummel, who was a key influencer in Victorian men's fashion and supposedly invented the cravat; Admiral Lord Nelson who famously led at the Battle of Trafalgar; Sir Winston Churchill; Charlie Chaplin; and Oscar Wilde.

It is also thought that James Benning, an eccentric member of the Lock family, inspired the Mad Hatter in Lewis Carroll's "Alice's Adventures in Wonderland". Lock and Co. are still independently owned and run by the Lock family.

Continue a few doors down to Berry Bros and under the façade's No 3 there is a small alleyway, head through the archway here (easily missed).

You now find yourself in Pickering Place (8), one of St James's hidden gems. This tiny courtyard is the smallest square in Britain, and it was supposedly also host to the last public duel in England. Before it was a courtyard, this was a small garden. Lord Palmerston (twice Prime Minister) was also once a resident here and there is a stone plaque commemorating this.

8

On your way back out look out for the plaque on the wall remembering that this was the location of the first Republic of Texas Legation (also known as the Texas embassy) between 1842 and 1845, when Texas joined the United States of America. The panels on the walls are supposedly originals from the Tudor period.

Back on St James's Street, take a look at the building that is attached to this alleyway.
Berry Bros and Rudd (9), established in 1698, is the oldest wine and spirit merchant in the country. It has the obligatory Royal Warrants: this time from Her Majesty, Queen Elizabeth II and her son, Prince Charles, Prince of Wales.

Originally established as a grocer by Elizabeth Pickering, it supplied the fashionable coffeehouses of the area
- the sign from the coffee mill still stands over the shop.
1698 was the year St. James's Palace had become the
official principal residence of the monarch so this was a
very fashionable location to set up shop.

Inside the shop they still have a set of set of weighing
scales which were used to weigh costumers well before
this was something that could be done in the comfort of
your own home.

The cellars beneath the wine shop date from the early 18th century. Louis Napoleon, later to
become Emperor Napoleon III, held clandestine meetings here during his exile in the 1840s,
plotting his return to France. Today these same gorgeous cellars host wine-tasting experiences.

The business is still owned and run by the Berry and Rudd families, whom give it its name.

Continue down to the junction.

The imposing building ahead across the road is the magnificent St. James's Palace (10), the
most senior royal palace in the United Kingdom. The palace was constructed between 1531
and 1536 in a red-brick Tudor style.

The palace was built on the site of a leper hospital dedicated to St James the Less, under the in-
struction of the notorious King Henry VIII, as a place to escape formal court life. At that time
it was secondary to the enormous Palace of Whitehall.

In the Stuart era (1603-1714), monarchs Charles II,
James II, Mary II and Anne were all born at the palace.
George I and George II used it as their primary London residence. However, George III found the house
too small and uncomfortable and purchased Buckingham House (precursor to Buckingham Palace) and
they increasingly began to use that residence instead.
By 1837, the move was officialised when Queen Victoria chose Buckingham Palace as her primary London
home.

Today St James's Palace is a working palace, and the
Royal Court is still formally based there, despite the monarch residing elsewhere. It is also the
London residence to some of the less high profile royals. These include: Princess Anne, Princess Royal (sister of Prince Charles and Prince Andrew); Princess Beatrice of York (daughter
of Prince Andrew and Sarah Ferguson); Princess Eugenie of York (daughter of Prince Andrew
and Sarah Ferguson); and Princess Alexandra (second cousin of Prince Philip).

The palace is used to host official receptions, such as those of visiting heads of state, and
charities of which members of the royal family are patrons. Various offices are also inside the
building including the Royal Collection Department, the Queen's Watermen, and Honourable
Corps of Gentlemen at Arms.

The street to the left is Pall Mall, which is famous for its gentlemen's clubs. The street's name
comes from a lawn game, which was a precursor to croquet, called "pall-mall" which was
played in the area in the 17th century. The game was introduced to England by James I and it
was already popular in France and Scotland. The street itself was built in 1661 under the rule of
Charles II, though a road has been on its site since at least the 11th century.

**Continue past the Quebec Government Offices to the Commonwealth Information Centre
and the Commonwealth Secretariat on the left.**

As we are focusing on royalty on this walk, it is pertinent to touch on the issue of the Commonwealth. The Commonwealth of Nations (established in 1949) is a collection of 52 independent states, the majority of which are former colonies of the British Empire. Member states have no legal obligation to one another. Instead, they are united by language, history, culture and their shared values of democracy, free speech, human rights, and the rule of law. The Head of the Commonwealth is the ruling monarch. Separately, The Queen is the ceremonial head of state and constitutional monarch of 16 members which form the Commonwealth realms.

The Secretariat supports Commonwealth member countries to achieve development, democracy and peace and was established in 1965.

Continue down Pall Mall.

Number 71 Pall Mall houses the Oxford and Cambridge Club (11), in a building dating from 1838 in a Greek Revival style. This private member's club accepts both men and women who are alumni or senior staff from Oxford and Cambridge universities.

At number 79, there is a blue heritage plaque remembering the home of Nell Gwyn (12) and one of the largest public scandals of its time. Nell Gwyn was one of many mistresses of King Charles II – legend has it that a tunnel connected Nell Gwynn's abode with St James's Palace, allowing the two to meet without being spotted in public together. The Crown Estate today owns almost the entirety of the area of St. James's with the exception of this building, which Nell Gwyn apparently convinced Charles to give her the land it stood on in 1676.

Cross back over the street and turn the first left into St. James's Square.

St James' Square was developed from the 1720s onwards and immediately became one of London's most fashionable addresses. There are a few notable buildings on the street and you may wish to do a loop of the square:

• No. 31 is Norfolk House (13) – the London residence of the Dukes of Norfolk for many generations. Also where U.S. General Dwight D. Eisenhower had his headquarters during World War II. Also of note is the statue of William III in the centre of the gardens.
• No. 4 is The Naval and Military Club ("The In & Out") [14] which is a private member's club accepting both men and women. This was also home of Nancy Astor, the first woman to sit as an MP in the House of Commons;
• No. 14 is home to the London Library (15) - the largest independent lending library in the world, having operated since 1840 with over 17 miles of bookshelves and 1 million items, don't let the small façade fool you;
• No. 16 is home to the East India Club (16) – a men's only club to this day, originally only for 'the servants of the East India Company and Commissioned Officers of Her Majesty's Army and Navy'.

Exit St James's Square via King Street to the west. Stay on the right-hand side of the road. On the corner ahead is Christie's (17) with it's red flags.

Christie's, a world-renowned auction house, was founded in London in 1766 by James Christie. The flagship King Street location has been Christie's home since 1823, though there are several Christie's locations around the world. In New York, in November 2017, a painting called "Salvator Mundi", attributed to Leonardo Di Vinci sold for a record $450.3 million.

In London, past sales have included: a copy of the black dress worn by Audrey Hepburn in the film "Breakfast at Tiffany's" sold for £467,200; a Bugatti Royale for a world record price of £5.5 million; and Rubens Old master Painting "Lot and his Daughters" sold for just under £44.9 million.

Take a right onto Duke Street St James's.

This area of St James's is filled with fine arts: art galleries, auction houses, silver dealers, antique sellers and rare book collections.

Continue north up Duke Street St James's to the corner with Jermyn Street.

Jermyn Street is synonymous with gentlemen's fashion, with a focus on British brands. The street is named after Henry Jermyn who developed this area close to St James's Palace.

Continue up Duke street St James until you reach Piccadilly.

You should be beside a turquoise colour-wrapped building called Fortnum and Mason (18), one of London's finest department stores (the colour is actually "eau de nil", not turquoise). Although, F&M is perhaps not as well known as Harrods or Selfridge's, it predates them by over 100 and 200 years respectively, being founded in 1707.

18

The legacy began in 1705 with Hugh Mason, from a small store in St James Market, and William Fortnum, who took a post as Footman in Queen Anne's household and stayed in Mr Mason's spare room.

The shop has introduced various food concepts to the UK over the years: In 1738, F&M created a portable food for long journeys – the world's first scotch egg: a hard-boiled egg wrapped in sausage meat and fried breadcrumbs. In 1886, a young entrepreneur – Henry J. Heinz from the USA – also convinced F&M to stock the first baked beans in the country.

You may wish to go inside the shop at this point to experience it: the ground-floor focuses on gifts and sweets, there are separate floors dedicated to men and women, there is an ice cream parlour, a food hall and wine bar in the basement, a café and even a tea room, unveiled by The Queen along with Camilla, Duchess of Cornwall and Catherine, Duchess of Cambridge. Be sure to look out for F&Ms famous hampers on the ground floor, ranging from £75 to £1000 – there's even a set of hampers called the Imperial Hamper retailing for £6000.

Fortnum and Mason holds warrants from The Queen and Prince Charles. However, in 2014, Fortnum and Mason was part of a scandal after falsely claiming that some meat in its stores was sourced from Royal Farms, after the Windsor Estate stopped supplier the shop after being constantly 'bullied' into cutting its prices.

Look up at the beautiful clock on Fortnum and Mason – you need to move away from the shop to see it clearly. Installed in 1964, the bells from the same foundry as Big Ben. Every 15 minutes a melody is played on eighteen bells, and once an hour figurines of Fortnum and Mason themselves appear to check that standards are being upkept.

Head East (right) along Piccadilly.

Immediately next door to F&M, is Hatchard (19), booksellers since 1797. The shop is proud to feature all three Royal Warrants and has occupied the current building at number 187 for over two centuries, making it London's oldest bookshop.

19

The shop's excellent relationship with authors means it holds many book signing events, and offers several first editions and pre-signed books for sale.

A few doors further down at number 195 Piccadilly is BAFTA (20), the British Academy of Film and Television Arts, which holds the BAFTA awards, similar to the Oscars.

Note the beautiful building above BAFTA's entrance which was originally home to the Royal Institute of Painters in Water Colours, a name which you can see carved towards the top of the buildings. There are also busts of famous paintings on the building, including notably JMW Turner, fourth from the left. This purpose built art gallery was in use from 1885 until the lease expired in 1970 – in 1976, BAFTA moved into the building.

Further down, the parade of shops gives way to the magnificent St. James's Church (21), which was designed by Christopher Wren (famous for St. Paul's Cathedral) and was consecrated in 1684. The church was severely damaged by enemy action in 1940, during the Second World War but has been lovingly restored. The poet William Blake was baptised here in 1757.

You may also find the small Piccadilly Market in the courtyard in front of the church. On Mondays and Tuesdays (11:00am to 5:00pm), the focus is on food and on Wednesdays to Saturdays (10:00am to 6:00pm), it is a crafts market. There is no market on Sunday.

Almost immediately after St. James's Church, take a right down Church Place.

Once back on Jermyn Street take a look at any black lamppost (22) with its gold details roughly at chest height – there are two symbols of the lamppost, one of which is an elaborate 'W' and another which closely resembles the Chanel logo. The "W" informs you that the land you are on is past of Westminster and the 'Chanel logo' is in fact two interlocking letter 'c's for "City Council", so the whole message is that this is a lamppost maintained by "Westminster City Council".

Take a left and follow Jermyn Street until you reach the much grander Regent Street St. James. From this corner you can see Piccadilly Circus to your left, which is not featured on this walk (see our West End walk). Instead turn right and head down the street, crossing over Charles II Street (you can't say London doesn't spoil you with historic street names) and the street is renamed Waterloo Place. Continue towards the column up ahead, and pause on the corner of Waterloo Place and Pall Mall.

22

23

In the traffic island to your left are a collection of statues forming The Guards Crimean War Memorial (23), commemorating the victory of the Allied Forces between 1853 and 1856.

The war was fought by the Ottoman Empire (broadly speaking, today's Turkey), France, Britain and Sardinia as part of the Allied Forces against the Russian Empire. The war initially was a religious battle with Russia promoting the rights of the Eastern Orthodox Church, and the French promoting those of the Roman Catholics; it then morphed into a territorial battle as the Russian Empire attempted to expand into the Ottoman Empire. The death toll totalled over 753,000 across both sides.

The memorial dates from 1861 and contains an allegorical figure at the top, originally called Honour (but today referred to as Victory) with her arms outstretched. Beneath her are three guardsmen. The bronze sculptures are melted cannons seized in Sevastopol, Soviet Union.

In 1914, the memorial was pushed back about 30 feet (10 m) to its current position so that two statues could be added in front. These are of Florence Nightingale (a nurse in the war, who later founded modern nursing by establishing the first secular nursing school in the world) on the left hand side, and Sidney Herbert (secretary at war) on the right.

Cross to the other side of Pall Mall to the large stucco building opposite and continue along Waterloo Place to the main entrance of the building ahead.

This large building on your right is the The Athenaeum (24), another gentlemen's club. Founded in 1824 by John Wilson Croker, the club accepts both men and women members with interests in science, engineering and literature.

24

The building was one of the earliest buildings ever to be lit by electric light, using its own generator until a public supply became available in the mid 1890s. Notable members have included: Decimus Burton (the clubhouse's architect), Michael Faraday, Charles Darwin, Charles Dickens, Sir Arthur Conan Doyle and Robert Louis Stevenson. In total, 52 members of the Club have won the Nobel Prize, including at least one in each category of the prize.

Above the main entrance is a statue of Athena (the Goddess of wisdom, craft, and war), who the club is named after.

In front of the club there are two blocks on the edge of the pavement by the roadside. This is a horse block which was used to aid mounting and dismounting from a horse. It was put here under orders from the Duke of Wellington in 1830. On the other side of the road, there is another one of these. Despite the many changes in payments and road styles over the years, these still remain.

Across Waterloo Place, is the Institute of Directors. Founded in 1904, this organisation is dedicated to business entrepreneurs and company directors. The building was formerly occupied by The United Service Club from 1828 until 1978, when it shut down after financial difficulties.

Immediately past the Athenaeum Club, on the right is the club's garden terrace where you can often see members enjoying themselves. There is also a statue of Sir Keith Park, a New Zealand Solider, who fought in WWI and WWII as a flying ace and RAF commander. The sculpture was placed here in 2010 for the 70th anniversary commemorations of the Battle of Britain, in which Park was in operational command, organising fighter patrols over France during the Dunkirk evacuation and the defence of London and southeast England.

Statues of Sir John Franklin and John Fox Burgoyne also feature on this side of the street. Franklin was the captain of two ships which left to voyage the last unnavigated section of the North-West passage (across the Arctic) in 1845. The expedition was lost and all men onboard are presumed to have died; despite this, Franklin was seen as a hero in Victorian times.

John Fox Burgoyne was a British Army officer who took part in the Siege of Malta and in numerous battles of the Peninsular War, including some under the Duke of Wellington. He notably also acted as an advisor during the Crimean War.

25

In the centre of Waterloo Place is a statue of Edward VII on Horseback, sculpted in 1924 and unveiled by his son George V.

Continue ahead to the enormous Duke of York Column (25). Walk down the steps ahead. Look back to fully appreciate the monument when reading the next section. Behind you the red-coloured road is The Mall, the processional route to and from Buckingham Palace, St. James's

The Duke of York Column is dedicated to Prince Frederick, Duke of York. Frederick was the commander-in-chief of the British Army during the French Revolutionary Wars, and helped restructure and modernise the army. He is immortalised in the nursery rhyme "The Grand Old Duke of York".

Being incredibly popular, when the Duke died in 1827, senior officers proposed a memorial which was paid for with one day's wages from all the soldiers who agreed to the measure.

Palace and Clarence House. This is prominently featured in royal weddings, the Queen's official birthday celebrations, coronations and other royal occasions with it being the route the monarch takes in a car or a carriage.

The detail in The Mall even extends to the lighting: The Mall has an underlying nautical theme ending at Trafalgar Square and Admiralty Arch to the east. For example, look at the black lampposts and you will find small back galleons on the top of each as if Nelson is surveying them from his column in Trafalgar Square nearby. The white tall retractable flagpoles are used during official occasions to add flags as decorations to The Mall.

To the left, with the Duke of York column behind you at the end of The Mall is Admiralty Arch, unveiled in 1912 and commissioned by King Edward VII in memory of his mother, Queen Victoria. The building was originally used as offices by the Admiralty. The building is currently leased to a private developer and will be transformed into flats, a hotel, a private members' club and restaurants. The 12,000 ft2 (1,100 m2) home will have 12 rooms and 12 bathrooms and be on sale for £150 million once complete.

Continue up The Mall away from Admiralty Arch, heading in the direction of Buckingham Palace visible at the end of the road ahead.

The big stucco building on your right after the Duke of York Steps is the rear of the Royal Society based inside Carlton House (26). Formed in 1660, the institution promotes, supports and recognises excellence in science. Previously Carlton House was home to the Embassy of Germany. The enormous building also houses the Royal Academy of Engineering.

Further up The Mall, on the right hand side there is a memorial to the Queen Mother and her husband George VI (27).

George reigned until his death in 1952 when Queen Elizabeth II became the monarch. George VI was the topic of popular movie The King's Speech due to his speech impediment. The Queen Mother's popularity cannot be understated: there was a 4-hour long wait to see her coffin lying-in-state in Westminster Hall.

27

Across The Mall is St. James's Park, dated from 1603, initially a private garden. Slightly further along The Mall, on the right is a large red building with a high wall and many flags. This is Marlborough House (28), the headquarters of the Commonwealth of Nations. It was originally completed in 1711 by Christopher Wren and was the London residence of the Dukes of Marlborough until 1817, when The Crown took it over.

Continue along The Mall, crossing Marlborough Road – you can see another view of St James's Palace (10) on your right, which we saw earlier on in the tour. After the palace, there is a small road with black gates – approach it.

This is the official entrance to Clarence House (29) – the white building to the right of the road, next to St James's Palace. The original Clarence House was designed by John Nash between 1825 and 1827 for the Duke of Clarence (later William IV) who found St. James's Palace too small.

Between 1953 and 2002, Clarence House was the residence of the Queen Mother. Upon her death, the house underwent a large refurbishment and only a small part of the original building remains. Since 2003, it has been home to Prince Charles and, more recently, also to his wife, Camilla.

Immediately next door to the left when looking at Clarence House is Lancaster House (30), more yellow in colour. This is mostly used as a conference and filming

30   29

ocation today: recent productions include Sherlock Holmes: A Game of Shadows, The King's Speech, and Netflix's "The Crown".

Behind the black gates, on the Clarence House side of the road you may be able to spot two of the famous Queen's Guards with their distinctive red uniforms and black hats (they wear a grey coat in the winter due to falling temperatures). The guards' hats (called "Bearskins") are to this day are by-products made of bear skin from Canadian bears culled to control their population. These men are most famous for guarding Buckingham Palace, but can also be found here at Clarence House, at the Tower of London and Windsor Castle.

The Queen's Guard are soldiers and their role is not purely ceremonial, despite popular belief. The Guards provide sentries throughout the day and night and they also patrol the grounds of the palaces. Regiments guard for a 24 to 72-hour period, with each individual soldier rotating between positions working for 2 hours, followed by a 4-hour rest period.

The switchover of regiments is marked by the Changing the Guard ceremony. One of the best positions to see this event is anywhere along The Mall between Clarence House and St. James's Palace – the ceremony takes place daily in the summer and up to 4 times a week outside of summer; aim to be on The Mall by 10:40am, as the guards leave St James Palace at 10:42am. The guard change ceremony will also feature either one or two bands. The entire ceremony is cancelled in very wet weather conditions.

The Queen's Guard can be made up of any guards from Commonwealth units trained for the post. However, the majority of the time, the Queen's Guard comes from one of five different foot guard regiments: Grenadier Guards, Coldstream Guards, Scots Guards, Irish Guards and Welsh Guards. The easy way to recognise them is by the coloured plumes in their hats: Grenadier (White), Coldstream (Red), Scots (No Plume), Irish (Blue) and Welsh (White and Green).

Continue up The Mall to Buckingham Palace (31).

Buckingham Palace started its life as Buckingham House in 1703, the Duke of Buckingham's London residence. In 1761, it was bought by King George III, for his wife (Queen Charlotte) and was known as The Queen's House.

The house was expanded to multiple times its original size in the 19th century with the principle architects being John Nash and Edward Blore. At one point, it even had an enormous archway marking the entrance (Marble Arch) roughly where today's white façade stands.

In 1837, Queen Victoria became the first monarch to use it as her London residence. The palace's expansion continued, as Marble Arch was moved to an area known at the time as Tyburn (approx. 1.5mi north –west of the palace), and the Eastern façade was built, which you see ahead of you. This is the most recognisable side of the palace containing the balcony used by the Royal Family during ceremonies. The Eastern front completed the quadrangle to create a courtyard in the centre.

Today, Buckingham Palace has 775 rooms in total, of which 19 are State rooms, 52 are Royal and guest bedrooms, 188 are staff bedrooms, 92 are offices and 78 are bathrooms. Buckingham Palace's gardens span 42 acres (slightly smaller than Green Park on the right).

The palace opens every summer to the public, for tours of the State Rooms and the gardens, when The Queen is at Balmoral Castle in Scotland for her summer break.

To check if the Queen is in residence, look up at the flagpole at the top of the palace – if it is the Union Flag, the Queen is not in residence; if it is a gold-red-blue flag (the Royal Standard), then the monarch is in residence.

At weekends, the Queen is usually at Windsor Castle. It is widely known that Queen Elizabeth

II thinks Buckingham Palace is too big and impersonal, and she and Prince Philip had initially wanted to live in Clarence House, having extensively refurbished it before her coronation.

Immediately in front of Buckingham Palace in the centre of the road is the Victoria Memorial (32), unveiled in 1911, but only fully completed in 1924. At the top in gilded bronze is Winged Victory, towards the bottom of the memorial (facing The Mall) is a statue of Queen Victoria on a throne, followed by statues representing Constancy, Courage, Motherhood, Justice and Truth. The sculptor Thomas Brock, choose these values as those Queen Victoria is remembered for.

At the corners further away are statues with lions representing Peace, Progress, Agriculture and Manufacture – strengths of the Victorian era. There are also fountains in the memorial and spread throughout are nautical symbols, commemorating the country's naval power.

Continue to the right towards the golden Canada Gates (33) **by Green Park.**

33

The Canada Gates were unveiled in 1911 as a present from Canada and are part of the Queen Victoria Memorial site. The gates feature the emblems of the seven Canadian provinces of the time and are similar to those used at the front of Buckingham Palace itself.

Continue around the gates to enter Green Park.

This 47-acre park is the smallest Royal Park in London and is the last section of the tour. Almost straight ahead after entering the park, slightly to the left, is the Canada Memorial (34) – it was unveiled in 1994 and commemorates members of the Canadian Forces who lost their lives in both World Wars. The memorial is sculpted in red granite and contains bronze maple leaves; water travels down the sculpture creating the illusion of the leaves floating.

Head towards Lancaster House as possible while staying in the park. Once there, turn left and take the pathway in the park walking north, passing Lancaster House on your right.

Green Park (35) gets its name as it has no official flower beds, no lakes, no permanent buildings and no playgrounds: it is green throughout. The popular explanation goes as so: This was once the private garden of St. James's Palace and was filled with flowers. On a Spring day, Charles II was walking through the garden with his wife Catherine when she asked him to pick a flower and give it to the most beautiful woman he knew. He picked a flower and gave it to a passing servant girl. Annoyed, Catherine stormed off to the palace and ordered that the gardeners rip out all the flowers. The tradition of no flowers continues to this day.

Continue north along the pathway. Soon on the right is Spencer House (36).

36

Spencer House, commissioned in 1756, is owned by Earl Spencer. The current Earl is Charles Spencer (Diana Spencer's brother). Spencer House is one of the last of the many aristocratic townhouses still intact in central London. Today it is used by a private company and for events. Public tours are held weekly, usually on Saturdays.

Continue north up the pathway.

If you are here during warmer weather, you will likely see deckchairs on the grass. On warm days, these will all be occupied. The cost is £1.80 per hour, payable to staff after sitting down.

Just before you exit Green Park, on the left by the food hut is the Diana Fountain (37) dedicated to Diana, the goddess of the hunt in Greek mythology.

The tour ends here, at the entrance of Green Park Station.

Walk 3: Westminster, Whitehall and the Government

Walk Length: 3.05km / 1.90 mi
Timings: 1h 45m (fast), 2h (regular), 2h 15m (leisurely)
Start: St James's Park station
End: Charing Cross station

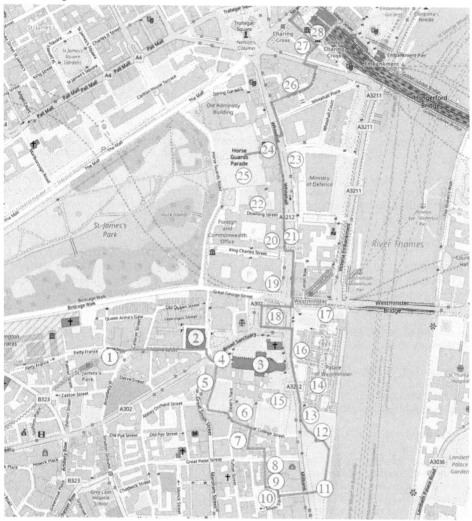

(1) 55 Broadway	(15) Jewel Tower
(2) Methodist Central Hall	(16) Oliver Cromwell
(3) Westminster Abbey	(17) Big Ben
(4) The Sanctuary	(18) Parliament Square
(5) Westminster Abbey Choir School	(19) Government Offices Gt. George St.
(6) Westminster School	(20) Foreign & Commonwealth Office
(7) Georgian Houses	(21) The Cenotaph
(8) Air Raid Shelters	(22) Downing Street
(9) Bricked Up Windows	(23) Banqueting House
(10) St. John's Church	(24) Horse Guards
(11) Buxton Memorial Fountain	(25) Horse Guards Parade
(12) The Burghers of Calais Monument	(26) Great Schotland Yard
(13) Emmeline Pankhurst	(27) Sherlock Holmes ub
(14) Houses of Parliament	(28) Benjamin Franklin House

Begin at St. James's Park Station. Use the exit with signs directing you towards "Park and Broadway". In the shopping centre above the station, follow signs for Westminster Abbey, Central Hall and QE Conference Centre. At the tube station on Broadway, head down Tothill Street towards Westminster abbey in the distance.

Once you have crossed into Tothill Street, take a moment to look back at the building above St. James's Park station. This is 55 Broadway (1), a 1920s art-deco inspired building designed by Charles Holden.

When it was completed in 1929, it was the tallest office block in the city and was the headquarters of the Underground Electric Railways Company of London, which ran the underground at the time. It was in use by Transport for London until 2017.

To the right, past 55 Broadway, is the distinctive shape of The Ministry of Justice, nicknamed "The Mushroom". Completed in 1976, it was previously the site of the Home Office until 2004.

Tothill Street gets its name from the name of the land here before it was developed Tothill Fields. In the 18th century it was home to Westminster Cricket club. The area later was also notorious for its towering prison and correctional facility (Tothill Fields Bridewell), which stood here from 1618 to 1884.

Walk towards Westminster Abbey.

On Tothill Street, just before the last building on the left, there is a small street called Matthew Parker Street. Matthew Parker was Archbishop of Canterbury (the spiritual leader of the country's religion, the Church of England) between 1559 and 1575. He apparently was also wanting to know the latest going on in the Church and gave rise to the phrase "Nosey Parker".

At the end of Tothill Street, you come to a large intersection with many crossing points. Take a look at Methodist Central Hall (2) **across the street on your left.**

Completed in 1911 as a Methodist church, it also houses a major conference centre with 22 meeting and conference rooms. It was in this building that the United Nations held its first General Assembly in 1946. There is also an excellent café/restaurant in the basement of Methodist Central Hall, as well as free, clean toilets.

Across the street ahead is Westminster Abbey (3)**. This is an excellent spot for a photo.**

Westminster Abbey's origins date back to 960 when Benedictine monks settled on the site. In the 11th century, Kind Edward the Confessor had St. Peter's Abbey built on the site in a Romanesque style as a burial church for himself. The building was consecrated in 1065, just one week before Edward's death. In 1066, William the Conqueror stormed the aisle of the Abbey and crowned himself king – the first recorded coronation in the Abbey.

By 1245, Henry III had begun the construction of the current church in an Anglo-French Gothic style – a replacement for the inadequate Norman church. By 1517, the majority of the church as we see it today was complete.

In the 1530s, Henry VIII reformed the church with the creation of the Church of England and the country's separation from Catholicism. During this period, known as the dissolution of the monasteries, Henry VIII made the monarch the head of the Church of England (this is still the case today) and seized land from the monasteries, thereby enriching himself. It also led to the destruction of hundreds of monasteries across the country. Westminster Abbey was granted the status of a Cathedral, sparing it from this fate.

The next major change to Westminster Abbey was the addition of the Western towers from 1722 to 1745, constructed of Portland Stone and designed by Nicholas Hawksmoor in a Gothic Revival style. These are the tower which face you today.

Today, the church is open to the public – services are free, whereas self-guided audio tours cost £22 per adult. Touring is not permitted on Sundays and other religious days. The Abbey has been home to 38 coronations of monarchs, and at least 16 royal weddings including more recently those of Queen Elizabeth II and Prince Philip, and Prince William and Catherine Middleton. It was also the location of Diana, Princess of Wales' funeral ceremony.

Cross to The Sanctuary (4), **the yellow building to the right of Westminster Abbey.**

4

The Sanctuary is composed of several buildings – this is number 4 and was designed by George Gilbert Scott in 1853. It houses offices today.

Standing in the middle of the road facing The Sanctuary and the Western façade of Westminster Abbey is a column which is a memorial to the boys of Westminster School who fought in the Russian/Crimean and Indian wars in the 1850s. At the top is a statue of St. George slaying a dragon. Beneath St. George are four seated monarchs – one facing in each direction (Edward the Confessor, Queen Elizabeth I, Henry III and Queen Victoria). The memorial was also designed by George Gilbert Scott.

Head through the archway with the barrier under The Sanctuary building to enter the secluded Dean's Yard. Despite the fact the entrance is manned, you do not need to ask security to go through on foot – you may simply walk through. Walk through towards the green square, looking back at the Abbey.

Dean's Yard dates from the time of the medieval abbey/monastery. This is an excellent place to admire the flying buttresses on the side of the abbey. There is also a group entrance to Westminster Abbey on one side.

Continue ahead into the square on the western side.

The large red brick building on the right is Westminster Abbey Choir School (5). This purpose-built school caters to a tiny cohort of students – about 30 boys who sing in the Westminster Abbey choir. At this most private of private schools, fees are heavily subsidised by the church and parents pay a 20% contribution towards the costs (£8,400 per year of the £42,000 a year fee).

5

Due to the intense schedule, this is a boarding only school – as well as education, the boys have choir practice at 8:15am and also sing Evensong at the Abbey at 5:00pm on most days. Although there is a thorough and varied curriculum, there is a particular focus on singing and music. The school caters to boys between the age of 8 and 13.

Continue round the square until you reach the corner opposite to that which you came in. There is a small passageway under a building which you should take. Once through, turn left onto and continue ahead on Great College Street. Notice the Victorian gas lamps still in use in this area.

The buildings on Great College street to the left are another school – Westminster School (6), not to be confused with the Westminster Choir School. This school does not receive funding from the Abbey. There are two parts to the school: the "Under School" for ages 7 to 13, and the School itself from ages 13 to 18.

The school dates back to at least the 14th century and possibly earlier. From ages 7 to 16 the school is boys only, and from then on girls are also accepted into the cohort. This private school is one of the most expensive in the country, with those who choose to board paying over £37,000 per year. Day pupils pay over £26,000. That price does pay for an excellent education: Westminster School achieved the highest percentage of students in the country accepted by Oxford and Cambridge colleges from 2002 to 2006.

Take a right onto Barton Street, an excellent example of a perfectly preserved area of Georgian houses (7), **and some are even 17th century.**

The attic room of Number 14 Barton Street, was the former home of writer, diplomat and archaeologist T.E. Lawrence. Number 6 was home to Lord Reith, in the 1920s, the first Director General of the BBC.

7

Take a left onto Cowley Street, following the road to the right. Cross over Great Peter Street and continue down Lord North Street towards the church ahead.

As you walk along Lord North Street notice how the houses have steps leading to the basement – many of these will have a faded mark of the letter 'S' followed by an arrow pointing down the steps on the brick walls. These were air raid shelters (8), which were much used during The Blitz in WWII.

8

On the corner of Lord North Street and Smith Square take a look at the buildings on either side on Lord North Street. Upon closer inspection you will see the bricked up windows (9).

This was likely due to the window tax. The tax was in place from 1696 to 1851, when it was repealed under the reign of Queen Victoria.

The tax was instituted in the reign of King William III as a progressive tax – the idea of an income tax was controversial, so instead a charge was placed upon windows in houses. The more windows you had, the wealthier you were likely to be.

9

When the tax was introduced, it had a base level of 2 shillings per house (approx. £13 in 2017) – you then paid for the number of windows you had. The first 9 were not charged; between 10 to 20 windows there was an extra annual charge of 4 shillings (approx. £26 in 2017) and for houses with more than 20 windows, there was an extra charge of 8 shillings (approx. £52 in 2017). The number of windows and charges changed during the lifetime of the tax. The tax was universally unpopular, being seen by some as a tax on "light and air".

A legal and easy way to avoid this tax was to reduce the number of windows you had, so many were bricked up with the window panes removed. This was usually done on the side of the house which would receive the least light throughout the day. The consequence of the tax lasting for over 150 years, was that many houses were also built with spaces for windows but filled with bricks from scratch.

The church ahead is St. John's (10) by architect Thomas Archer and completed in 1728. It was part of the government's proposal to build 50 new churches, though this goal was never accomplished. This was the most expensive of the churches built at the time, costing over £40,000.

The church is unusually nicknamed "Queen Anne's Footstool" – the story goes that when Archer was designing the church he asked the Queen what she wanted it to look like. She pushed over her footstool and said "Like that!", inspiring the building's four corner towers. Charles Dickens was not a fan calling it "a very hideous church" and describing it as "resembling some petrified monster, frightful and gigantic".

10

Although the baroque exterior survives, the original interior no longer exists: there was a fire in the 1740s, it was substantially refurbished in the 1820s and was a victim of The Blitz in the 1940s. It was later converted into a classical music concert venue, which is still in use.

The church has a café and restaurant, aptly named The Footstool, which may be a good place to rest and recharge. At the time of writing, the café is open weekdays from 8:30am to 5:00pm.

Head clockwise (left) around the church, exiting the square via Dean Stanley Street. Head down Dean Stanley Street, using the pedestrian crossing to cross Millbank and entering Victoria Tower Gardens. Continue ahead to the beautiful Buxton Memorial Fountain (11).

The Buxton Memorial Fountain commemorates the emancipation of slaves in the British Empire in 1834. It originally stood on Parliament Square in front of the Houses of Parliament and dates back to 1866. The whole process of the abolition of the slave trade began with the Slave Trade Act in 1807, but slave trading was only fully outlawed throughout the British Empire with the Slavery Abolition Act 1833, which came into force in August 1834.

Past the fountain, take a left down the pathway alongside the River Thames. There are some benches here if you need a rest. Continue down this path towards the Houses of Parliament. Where a pathway veers to the left take it to The Burghers of Calais Monument (12).

This sculpture, originally entitled "Les Bourgeois de Calais" was cast by Auguste Rodin and dates from the 1880s. It commemorates when the port of Calais in France was under siege by the English between September 1346 and August 1347 as part of the Hundred Years' War.

11

It specifically remembers the six citizens of Calais who offered themselves as hostage to Edward III; their lives were supposedly spared at the request of Edward's wife Philippa of Hainault. There are several casts of this sculpture around the world, including in Calais itself, as well as Paris, Copenhagen and even in Tokyo.

Continue heading north towards the Palace of Westminster's tower, looking for an exit. Before exiting you will find a monument to Emmeline Pankhurst (13).

12

Emmeline Pankhurst was the leader of the suffragette's movement that fought for the women's right to vote, particularly in the Victorian era. Eventually, in 1918, the government passed the Representation of the People Act 1918, allowing all men, as well as all women over the age of 30 who met minimum property qualifications the right to vote.
In 1928, the same year of Pankhurst's death another significant milestone was accomplished, with the passing of the Representation of the People (Equal Franchise) Act giving the vote to all women over the age of 21 on equal terms with men.

In 1999 Time magazine named Pankhurst one of the 100 Most Important People of the 20th Century. Along the wall on the right you will also find a plaque and inscription commemorating Emmeline's daughter, Christabel, who was also key to the suffragette movement.

Exit the park back onto Millbank/Abingdon Street. Turn right and walk to the base of the Victoria Tower, part of the Houses of Parliament (14).

The Palace of Westminster, containing the Houses of Parliament, is home to the UK parliament, and is the meeting place of the House of Commons and the House of Lords.

13

Before it was used by the government, this was the site of a royal palace in the 11th century and was the main residence of the monarch until a fire destroyed most of the complex in 1512. The building also began to be used by Parliament from the 13th century. After the fire, the complex was rebuilt, only be destroyed by an even bigger fire in 1834 – only a few small sections survived.

Charles Barry was commissioned to rebuild the Houses of Parliament which we see today in a Gothic Revival style. The palace today spans 8 acres and contains over 1,100 rooms. The palace's reconstruction began in 1840 and lasted over 30 years; interior works continued into the 20th century.

14

The Houses of Parliament is split into two halves: the House of Commons and the House of Lords. Here's how the political system works in this country: The House of Commons' Members of Parliament (MPs) are democratically elected by constituents who elect their local MP to represent them. There are 650 MPs at present, one for roughly every 92,000 in the country. The UK uses the "first-past-the-post" system in which the candidate with the most votes gets a seat to represent their constituency, and then the political party with the most seats forms the government and their leader becomes the Prime Minister. If the election results in no single party having a majority, then there is a hung parliament. In this case, the options for forming the government are either a minority government or a coalition.

Members of the House of Lords are appointed (except 90 hereditary peers elected among themselves, plus two others). The Lords includes 26 bishops from the Church of England, for example. There are not a fixed number of members of the House of Lords and at the time of writing in early 2018, there are about 800 – more than in the House of Commons. The House of Lords' key job is to scrutinise and suggesting amendments to bills approved by the House of Commons.

Uniquely, when voting members in both houses do not physically write down their votes on bills. Instead they physical enter one of two lobbies to say whether they agree or disagree with a bill and are counted on the way out. These counts determine the outcome of a vote. Ultimately, all bills are sent to the monarch for Royal Assent – without the signature of the monarch, a law cannot be passed.

Although Big Ben's clock tower is undoubtedly the most famous part of the Houses of Parliament, the Victoria Tower above you is often unappreciated. The archway here is the ceremonial entrance to the House of Lords, known as the Sovereign's Entrance. This is used by The Queen during The State Opening of Parliament. The tower above was built as a fire-proof safe for documents after the two previous fires on the site – this is known as the Parliamentary Archives and today houses over 3 million items. The archives are open to the public on weekdays at no charge with prior appointment.

Across the road is the Jewel Tower (15), part of the original Palace of Westminster.

It dates back to the 14th century. Its original purpose was to house the treasure of Edward III – at the time it was surrounded by a moat to prevent theft. It housed the monarchs' treasure until 1512 when Henry VIII was forced to relocate to Whitehall after the first fire. By the late 16th century it was used as storage for records from the House of Lords. Today, the Jewel Tower is open to the public as a small paid museum with archaeological exhibits.

15

Walk up Abingdon Street with the Houses of Parliament on your right.

Soon on the other side of the road, to the left you will be able to see the flying buttresses of Westminster Abbey and the Lady Chapel, paid for by funds in Henry VII's will – a lesser-known side to the church compared to the famous West Towers. A white statue of King George V (the grandfather of the current queen) stands in the courtyard in front.

On the right hand side, there is a black equestrian statue from 1856 of Richard I with his sword raised. Also known as Richard the Lionheart, Richard reigned as King of England between 1189 and 1199. Richard gained his nickname for his reputation as a military leader, crusading and protecting his landholdings in France.

Continue past the public entrance to the Houses of Parliament (the building is open for tours on select days) until you reach the statue of Oliver Cromwell (16) on the right.

Oliver Cromwell was a key member of an anti-monarchy coup and one of the signatories of King Charles I's death warrant in 1649. For a period of almost five years after the abolition of the monarchy, Cromwell acted as Lord Protector of the Commonwealth of England, Scotland, and Ireland. During his tenure he managed to, among other things, ban Christmas as it was considered a pagan festival.

Upon his death, Oliver Cromwell was buried in Westminster Abbey. In 1660 when the monarchy was restored, Royalists dug up his body and subjected him to a posthumous execution. After decapitating him, Cromwell's head was displayed

16

on a pole outside Westminster Hall (not too far from the spot you're standing in) until 1685, when it fell down in a storm.

If you follow the eye line of Cromwell's statue to St. Margaret's Church across the road you will see a bust of Charles I, the man who Cromwell helped execute – the two are stuck in history's ultimate staring contest. St. Margaret's itself was founded in the 12th century, but this incarnation of the church dates from 1523.

The building behind Oliver Cromwell is Westminster Hall, the oldest part of the Palace of Westminster which survived both fires and dates from 1097. Westminster Hall was the site of coronation banquets celebrating the new monarch from the 12th century to 1821. It is also where, after the death of royal or other significant figures, they lie in state with public access. The last time this was done was in 2002 upon the death of the Queen Mother: at one point there was a 4-mile queue of visitors paying their respects and seeing her coffin lying-in-state.

One cannot mention the Palace of Westminster without speaking about Big Ben (17). First of all, Big Ben is the name of the bell. The tower which most people call Big Ben is actually the Elizabeth Tower, standing at 316 ft tall (96 m), and the tallest four-faced chiming clock tower in the world. The tower dates from 1859 after the Palace of Westminster's second fire.

Big Ben (the bell) weighs in at 13.5 tons; four other bells are used for the chimes. The chimes play every 15 minutes and Big Ben on the hour. Big Ben is undergoing a £61 million refurbishment until 2021. The bells are silenced until then and The Elizabeth Tower itself will be covered in scaffolding for much of this time.

Despite its official name as the Elizabeth Tower, the vast majority of Londoners and visitors from around the world use the name Big Ben. It is unclear where the bell's name comes from, though there are two probable explanations: the bell may have been named after Benjamin Caunt – a well known boxer at the time - whose nickname was "Big Ben"; alternatively, and rather more plausibly, it may be named after Sir Benjamin Hall, who oversaw the installation of the bell.

Ahead on Parliament Square cross into the traffic island in the centre. Walk clockwise away from the Palace of Westminster on the traffic island to the next corner.

Across the road is Middlesex Guildhall, dating from 1913 and designed by J. S. Gibson. Today it houses Supreme Court of the United Kingdom, the highest appeal court in the land.

17

Back on Parliament Square (18), there are a plethora of statues, you may wish to read them all or skip to those of figures you are interested in (here statues are listed in a clockwise order):
• **Nelson Mandela**, President of South Africa from 1994 to 1999, anti-apartheid revolutionary and philanthropist.
• **Sir Robert Peel**, Prime Minister of the UK from 1841 to 1846. He also is famous for establishing the Metropolitan Police, the first modern police force; the nickname for police in the UK is "bobbies" after Sir Robert.
• **Mahatma Gandhi**, leader of the Indian independence movement
• **Benjamin Disraeli**, twice Prime Minister of the UK and close friend of Queen Victoria
• **Edward Smith Stanley**, three-time Prime minister of the UK, fought and succeeded to allow working class men to vote.
• **Henry John Temple**, 3rd Viscount Palmerston, spend nearly 58 years in high office in the government, was twice Prime Minister of the UK and was Foreign Secretary three times when Britain was at the height of its power. Distrusted by Queen Victoria.
• **Jan Smuts**, twice Prime Minister of South Africa, originally advocated racial segregation but soon changed his mind; helped found the organisation that became the Royal Air Force in Britain; part of Churchill's Imperial War Cabinet; the only man to sign both peace treaties ending the First and Second World Wars.
• **David Lloyd George**, Chancellor of the Exchequer from 1908 to 1915 – instrumental in helping lay foundations to found the welfare state, Prime Minister of the UK from 1916 to 1922; Secretary of State for War in 1916;
• **Sir Winston Churchill**, twice Prime Minister of the UK including during WWII – his speeches and broadcasts helped inspire British resistance; named the Greatest Briton of all time in a 2002 poll and one of Britain's most influential figures.

A new statue will also be unveiled in 2018 dedicated to Millicent Fawcett who founded the National Union of Women's Suffrage Societies in 1897, which ultimately led to the suffragette movement led by Emmeline Pankhurst (seen earlier in the tour). It will be the first statue of a woman on the square, and celebrates 100 years since women gained the right to vote. The statue will hold a placard reading "courage calls to courage everywhere" from a speech she gave. Dame Millicent died in 1929, a year after women were granted the vote on equal terms to men.

After the statue of Churchill, cross to the side of the Houses of Parliament, then cross again and head down Parliament Street/Whitehall. Across the road is a large white building.

The building is called Government Offices Great George Street (19), designed by John Brydon, and was completed in 1917. The building houses Her Majesty's Revenue and Customs (the tax office), HM Treasury and other government offices.

The basement of the building houses the Imperial War Museum, one of the most fascinating museums in London. It was the site of the Cabinet War Rooms including living quarters, map rooms and planning rooms from which Churchill, his Cabinet and the rest of his team ran the British side of WWII. This is now open to the public with the entrance on the other side of the building, facing St. James's Park.

Continue ahead until you reach the Red Lion pub.

19

The site of the Red Lion has housed a tavern since 1434 called Hopping Hall. The current building dates from the 1890s and was once a common haunt of Prime Ministers. Edward Heath, Winston Churchill and Clement Attlee were all known to stop here. If you are in need of a toilet break, these can be found upstairs on the first floor up a very steep staircase – the doors to the toilets are modelled after number 10 and 11 Downing Street's famous black doors.

Cross to the other side of the road using the pedestrian crossing just after the pub.

The enormous building, just after the HMRC building is the **Foreign and Commonwealth Office (20)**. The building dates from 1868 and was designed by George Gilbert Scott in an Italianate style. The building is open to the public on Open House Weekend each September and is beautiful inside.

Continue up Parliament Street which now becomes known as Whitehall.

In the centre of the road to the right is The Cenotaph (21) unveiled in 1920 and designed by Edwin Lutyens. Each year, on Remembrance Sunday (the Sunday closest to 11th November) a remembrance service takes place here to honour the war dead. Members of the royal family, the Prime Minister and other key figures in Britain lay wreaths of poppies at the base of the Cenotaph.

The symbol of the poppy stems from war itself. In 1915, after losing a friend in Ypres, Lieutenant Colonel John McCrae was inspired by poppies growing in battle-scarred fields to write the poem "In Flanders Fields". After the First World War, the poppy was adopted as a symbol of Remembrance.

Continue ahead along Whitehall until you reach some black gates on your left. This is Downing Street (22).

21

The street dates back to the 1680s when it was laid out on behalf of George Downing – at the time there were between 15 and 20 houses, designed by famed architect Christopher Wren. At that time, these gates did not exist and anyone could walk down into the cul-de-sac.

The left side of the street's houses were acquired by the government in the 1820s to construct the building that now houses the Foreign and Commonwealth Office. Barriers were placed in the 1970s, and security was increase twice in the 1980s due to mounting security concerns.

22

Since 1735, the key building has no doubt been Number 10 Downing Street on the right hand side of the road with a lantern outside (and often a policeman too) – this is the Prime Minister's office and official residence. Number 11 has been the official residence of the Chancellor of the Exchequer (the person responsible for public spending) since 1828, Number 12 is home to the Prime Minister's Press Office, and Number 9 is an entrance to the Privy Council Office (advisers to the monarch) and houses the Department for Exiting the European Union.

Continue up Whitehall past Downing Street. Soon on the right hand side you will see flag-poles out onto the street at Banqueting House (23).

The Banqueting House is the only surviving section of an enormous palace which once stood on this site – The Palace of Whitehall (hence this road's name). The palace had over 1,500 rooms (almost twice the size of today's Buckingham Palace) and was the main London residence of the English monarchs from 1530 until 1698 when it burnt down.

Banqueting House itself dates from 1622 and was designed by Inigo Jones with a beautiful ceiling painted by Rubens. The Banqueting House was designed to be used for entertainment - not purely "banquets", though meals would certainly have been served here as part of the entertainment. The hall's main use was for masques - a sophisticated blend of poetry, propaganda, music, dance and outlandish costume, and the King and Queen sometimes took part.

It was here from the windows on the first floor that Charles I stepped onto a scaffold on the afternoon of 30 January 1649 at 2:00pm for his execution. On that cold winter day, he wore two shirts to make sure the crowd did not think he was shivering from fear.

Today Banqueting House is an events venue but it is also open during the day to visitors. It is a true gem - though a small attraction with just 2 main areas (the basement and the main room), the ceiling alone is worth the small admission price for art and history buffs.

Further on the left is see a white building with a small courtyard called Horse Guards (24).

The current Horse Guards buildings date from 1759. The originals were commissioned in 1652 by Charles II – it was used to house the King's Guard and stabled over 100 horses when he lived at the Palace of Whitehall.

Following the palace's fire in 1698, the monarch moved to St James's Palace and Horse Guards was used as an entrance-way guarding the newly rehoused king. Horse Guards began to be used as offices as well. George III commissioned the current building in the Palladian style, which kept the same layout but doubled the interior space.

Today the building houses military offices, the Household Cavalry museum (paid admission) and still acts as the official ceremonial entrance to Buckingham Palace and St James's Palace, hence why it is guarded by two mounted sentries. The sentries still control vehicular access to this day, barring entry to anyone not a member of the Royal Family or unable to produce an Ivory Pass granting entry.

The sentries are on mounted duty between 10:00am and 4:00pm daily, from 4:00pm to 8:00pm there are two dismounted sentries, and overnight there is one dismounted sentry - the gates are locked at night. The sentries have performed this duty since 1660.

Walk into the courtyard through the gates, before you walk under the archways look left and right to see two dismounted guards.

This small courtyard is where the dismounting ceremony (the Four 'o' Clock Parade) takes place daily at 4:00pm. The inspection dates back to 1894 when Queen Victoria found the Horse Guards drinking and gambling instead of guarding her palace – as punishment, she vowed they would be inspected at 4:00pm daily for the next 100 years. The tradition continues today.

The clock at the top of the building has a black mark by the roman number 'II' remembering that 2:00pm was the time that Charles I was beheaded opposite at Whitehall Palace in 1649 – a black mark in the history of the nation.

Walk through under the archways where you come to the large Horse Guards Parade (25).

This parade ground was formerly where jousting tournaments were held when the complex was still part of the Palace of Whitehall. Here, daily at 11:00am (10:00am on Sundays), the Changing of the Queen's Life Guard ceremony takes place.

Facing St. James's Park to your right the red and white building with the green turret roofs is the Old Admiralty dating from the early 1900s. Immediately after it, a brown-coloured is the Admiralty Citadel, a bomb-proof operations shelter from 1941.

Head back onto Whitehall. Turn left, cross the road and continue up Whitehall. Take the second road on your right – Great Scotland Yard (26).

Great Scotland Yard is most famous for being the location of the first police commissioner's office. Technically the main entrance was on Whitehall, but it is the name of the back entrance (Great Scotland Yard) which became synonymous with the Metropolitan Police Force. The origin of the "Scotland" part of the street name is not clear, though it has been claimed that the street is where Scottish representatives stayed while visiting London. The Met have now moved to near the Houses of Parliament, though the police stables are still based on this road.

Head down Great Scotland Yard and follow the road round until you reach Northumberland Avenue. Here, use the pedestrian crossing on the left to get to the other side. Just round the corner to the left on Northumberland Street is the Sherlock Holmes pub (27).

The story of the Sherlock Holmes pub begins in 1951 at the Festival of Britain, a celebration of all things British with the aim to get the country's men and women upbeat after WWII. At this festival there was an exhibition on Sherlock Holmes, the fictional character from Sir Arthur Conan Doyle's series of books.

In 1957, the owners of the Northumberland Arms – the previous name of this pub – purchased the collection of items from the 1951 exhibition and moved them here. Today, the upstairs part of the pub has been converted until a recreation of Sherlock's flat which anyone can visit, and includes a restaurant area. The ground floor is

also filled with Sherlock memorabilia which has been accumulated over the year. This is a good place to make a stop for a drink or a meal with atmosphere as it is the second to last location on this walk.

Continue down Crown Passage to the right of the pub to Craven Street. Turn left.

After turning left, just a few doors down on your right is Benjamin Franklin House (28) at number 36 Craven Street – an amazing hidden gem, particularly for anyone looking for American heritage in the city. It is the only surviving former residence in the world of Benjamin Franklin, one of the American founding fathers. The house dates back to the 1730s and Franklin worked and lived there for 16 years.

Most of the house today is rather bare, so this museum is toured with live guides only to bring the history to life. The best tour, in our opinion, is the Historical Experience tour which runs from Wednesday to Sunday at set times; an Architectural Tour is available on Mondays.

This is the last stop. The nearest tube station is Charing Cross - turn right at the end of Craven Street ahead and you will see the station in less than 20 metres on your right.

Walk 4: The West End/Theatreland

Walk Length: 4 km / 2.5 mi
Timings: 2h (fast), 2h 30m (regular), 2h 45m (leisurely)
Start: Charing Cross station
End: Tottenham Court Road station

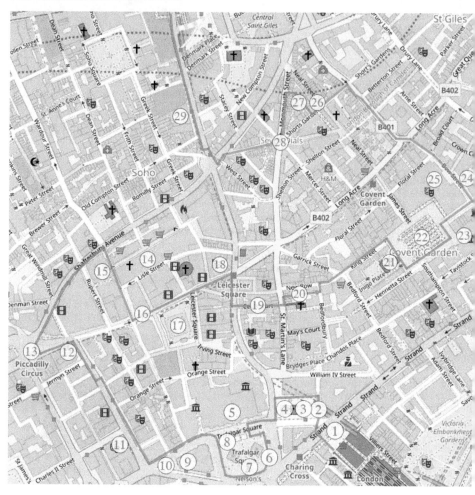

(1) Eleanor Cross
(2) A Conversation with Oscar Wilde
(3) East Window
(4) St. Martin in the Fields church
(5) National Gallery
(6) Smallest Police Station
(7) Nelson's Column
(8) Fourth Plinth
(9) Oceanic House
(10) Statue of George III
(11) Her Majesty's Theatre
(12) The Four Bronze Horses of Helios
(13) Piccadilly Circus
(14) Chinatown
(15) Wong Kei's

(16) Swiss Glockenspiel
(17) Leicester Square
(18) The Hippodrome
(19) Cecil's Court
(20) Goodwin's Court
(21) St. Paul's Church
(22) Covent Garden Plaza
(23) London Transport Museum
(24) Theatre Royal Drury Lane
(25) Royal Opera House
(26) Neal's Yard Water Clock
(27) Neal's Yard
(28) Seven Dials
(29) Foyles

This tour begins at Charing Cross station. Follow the signs to Charing Cross National Rail Station when leaving the tube. Once at the National Rail station use Exit 1 (Strand).

Ahead is the Eleanor Cross (1). The Eleanor Crosses were 12 stone monuments placed throughout east England in the 1290s. The crosses were memorials to Edward I's wife, Eleanor of Castille who had died in 1290. Her funeral cortège started in Lincoln and ending in Charing (in London), taking 12 nights to reach London. Each stopover point where the cortège rested had a memorial built there. Hence how Charing became Charing Cross.

The original Cross was slightly further up the road at the end of Whitehall, and was destroyed in 1647 under the order of the government. The current Eleanor Cross here is similar to the old cross, but more elaborate in style and dates from 1865. It was commissioned as a landmark for the opening of the Charing Cross Hotel (now the Amba Hotel). The area's name of Charing likely comes from the Anglo-Saxon word cerring, which means a bend; in this case the bend of the River Thames near here.

The major road running in front of the station is Strand. Strand means "beach" or "foreshore" in German; this became "Strond" in Old English, meaning the edge of a river.

Cross Strand, go up Duncanon Street ahead and take a right along the tree-lined Adelaide Street running along the back of the church.

Here you will find a bronze and granite sculpture called "A Conversation with Oscar Wilde" (2), designed as a bench so you can sit and 'chat' with the writer. It was the first public monument to Oscar Wilde outside of Ireland, and was unveiled in 1998.

Take a left alongside St. Martin in the Fields Church. Look at the unusual window at the back of the Church.

Known as East Window (3), this is actually an art installation by Iranian artist Shirazeh Houshiary. It was installed to replace a window destroyed by a bomb in WWII. Its unusual design is very modern when juxtaposed with the classical nature of the church, and the warping around a circle creates the impression of a cross with the lines.

Continue ahead alongside the church to the glass structure, the entrance to the Crypt of the St. Martin in the Fields.

Today this is an underground café-canteen style location, whereas the food is unremarkable, the setting and architecture are amazing. Do take a moment to go inside and see the original brick-vaulted ceilings and historic tombstones lining the floor.

Continue past the church and turn left for the main entrance - feel free to go inside if you wish. Admission is free. Alternatively, you can access the church from the Crypt Café.

The current St. Martin in the Fields church (4) building dates from 1726, designed by James Gibbs in a neoclassical style, though a church has stood on this site since at least the 13th century. The name "in the fields" remembers a time when the church was neither in the City of London, nor in the City of Westminster – it was in the middle of the countryside, rather than on the corner of one of London's most famous squares like it is today. Despite being an unpopular design at the time, the church was cloned around the world, particularly in the United States, as well as in locations as far-flung as India. The church is also famous around the world for its orchestra.

4

Above the famous portico, in the pediment, you can see the Royal coat of arms as this is the parish church to Buckingham Palace. Looking up at the crest, it is worth pointing out some details – the two main animals which make up the crest are a lion on the left and a unicorn on the right. These animals represent the two kingdoms which made up the United Kingdom when each had a separate royal family: the lion represents England and the unicorn represents Scotland. In 1603, James VI of Scotland inherited the English and Irish thrones, created one ruling Royal Family with one Royal coat of arms. Scotland uses a very similar coat of arms but gives more prominence to the unicorn, putting it on the left as well as other small changes.

Cross to the other side of the street onto Trafalgar Square.

Trafalgar Square commemorates the Battle of Trafalgar in 1805, where the British Royal Navy fought the combined French and Spanish Navies. The battle saw the British outnumbered 27 ships to 33 yet, under the leadership of Admiral Lord Nelson, victory was for the British, largely due to his strategic planning. The British did not lose a single ship during the battle.

Today, Nelson is honoured with the 169-foot (52m) tall Nelson's Column which dominates the square and dates from 1843. A statue of Nelson is at the top. The column, pedestal and statue combined are purportedly the same height as Nelson's ship, HMS Victory.

In this section of the walk, we will be working our way around Trafalgar Square clockwise.

Dominating the square on the north side is the magnificent National Gallery (5); the permanent collection is free admission and you could easily spend several afternoons inside with its 2300 paintings to see. Some of the most well-known works of art inside are Van Gogh's Sunflowers and Bathers at Asnières by Georges Seurat.

5

Over two-thirds of the paintings were private donations. It is well worth a visit. The building that houses the gallery dates from 1838 and was designed by William Wilkins.

Head down the steps by the equestrian statue of George IV (the king who moved his mews from this site to Buckingham Palace). Head across the square passing the fountains.

The centrepieces of these fountains were designed by Edwin Lutyens in the 1930s. The next statue on a plinth is Major General Sit Henry Havelock, who is remembered for his recapture of Cawnpore from rebels during the Indian Mutiny of 1857.

6

While facing this statue head-on, take a look to the right for an often-missed gem.

Before the pedestrian crossing on the square, there is a circular structure with a black lantern on top. This was supposedly the site of the world's smallest police station (6) – a policeman would enter through the small black door and have space for himself, a telephone to call Scotland Yard if necessary, and an all important kettle to make himself a cup of tea as necessary. The lamp at the top would flash in the event of trouble, which Trafalgar Square was known for, being the place for public gatherings – it still is often used during protests today. Today the structure is used for storing cleaning apparatus.

Walk towards the base of Nelson's column, so you are facing the column with the National Gallery in the background. Before delving into more depth about the column, turn back to look down Whitehall for one of the best views (and photos) of Big Ben in the distance, with an equestrian statue of King Charles I in the foreground – this statue marks the centrepoint of London today.

Now, take a look back at Nelson's Column (7).

The bronze reliefs on the pedestal of Nelson's column remember his naval battles. The one facing Whitehall and the statue of Charles I depicts Nelson dying after his victory at Cape Trafalgar, the other reliefs going clockwise depict battles at: St. Vincent, the Nile and Copenhagen.

The famous lions guarding the column also have an interesting story. Edwin Landseer the sculptor of the lions wanted his depiction of lions to be as accurate as possible, so he obtained a dead lion from London Zoo – as time went on and the real lion decomposed, the sculptures had to be improvised. The paws on the lion look too cat-like to have been inspired by a real animal, and many even say the rear legs look more like a dog than a lion, with some people claiming Landseer based the lions on his pet Labrador, earning them the nickname of "labra-lions".

Continue on your clockwise tour of Trafalgar Square to another statue.

This is Charles James Napier, who was the British Army's Commander-in-Chief in India from 1849 to 1851. His most significant milestone was conquering Sindh in Pakistan.

Continue towards the National Gallery, going up the steps to the final statue on the square. This is the Fourth Plinth (8).

The Fourth Plinth remained empty for over 150 years until 1999, when it was decided that the plinth would be used for temporary artworks. Over the years there has been a model of HMS Victory in a bottle, a boy on a rocking horse, and at the time of writing there is a giant thumbs up called "Really Good" – sculptures change every 18 to 24 months.

8

Coming in 2018 is a recreation of a winged bull that stood in Iraq for over 2700 years, which was destroyed by Isis in 2015 – the sculpture will be made out of empty date syrup cans. This will be followed in 2020 by "The End" which will be a sculpture of whipped cream with a drone, a cherry and a fly on top. A commonly held belief is that the plinth will feature a permanent statue of Queen Elizabeth II in the future, after Prince Charles succeeds her.

Perhaps the most unique exhibit took place in 2009 and was called "One and Other" where every hour, 24 hours a day, for 100 days straight, a different person took to the Plinth and could do whatever they wanted. A total of 2400 people took part.

Continue to the north part of the square by the National Gallery and take a left onto Pall Mall East, passing the Canadian High Commission on your left and the National Gallery

Sainsbury Wing on your right. Immediately after the Canadian High commission where the flags stop is Oceanic House (9).

Oceanic House was the London headquarters of the White Star Line, one of the premier shipping companies of its day. This is where they sold tickets to upcoming cruises, including the RMS Titanic, which sank just 5 days after being launched on its maiden voyage.

Ahead, in the middle of a traffic island, is an equestrian statue of George III (10), also known as 'The Mad' King George.

King George III suffered from an illness which we think today to be porphyria; he became mentally unstable and was not able to rule the country. He is also known as the king who lost America. Due to his mental instability, a regency was formed where his son took over and ruled on his behalf from 1811 to 1820.

Upon the death of his father, the Prince Regent became George IV. The Regency era became known as an age of great expansion in London with elaborate often Palladian-style architecture and the master-planning of great parts of London such as Regent's Park and Regent Street.

Take the next right onto Haymarket.

Haymarket's name dates from the Elizabethan era when it was used for the sale of hay, animal feed, horses and other animals as it was close to the Royal Mews at the time. It also marks the beginning of London's theatre district, the West End or Theatreland – on many of the street signs in this area you will see a black or red bar at the top attesting to this. The West End is the largest English-speaking theatre district in the world with 38 theatres and 41,600 seats to fill.

Continue up Haymarket until you reach two theatres.

On the right hand side of the road is the Theatre Royal Haymarket, the third-oldest working theatre in London dating back to 1720, though the current building was redesigned in 1821.

Across the street is Her Majesty's Theatre (11), one of London's buildings that changes its name according to the gender of the monarch.

It has been home to musical Phantom of the Opera since 1986. The current building dates from 1897, though the theatre's origins go back to the early 18th century.

Haymarket was where Burberry opened its first London shop in 1891. The brand moved into number 18-21 (a large white building with columns and archways on the face, a few doors down from Theatre Royal Haymarket) in 1913; this also became its headquarters, until 2007 when the company moved to another location not too far from Big Ben.

Continue up Haymarket. At the top of the hill, cross the road and turn left, where you will find The Four Bronze Horses of Helios (12) **on the corner.**

The statue depicts Aethon, Eos, Phlegon, and Pyrois, the four horses of Helios, Greek god of the sun. On the top of the building (you will need to look at these from a distance) are Helio's often overlooked three daughters, "The Three Graces". Both sets of statues are by Rudy Weller.

Continue left at this corner towards the centre of Piccadilly Circus (13).

Piccadilly Circus' most famous part is undoubtedly the electric billboard signs on the corner, which have existed since
1908. Previously, almost all the buildings on every part of
Piccadilly Circus were covered in these electric lights around
the circus and these were some of the first outdoor electric
lights anywhere in the world.

Today the advertisement are confined to just one building. The signs have been changed
multiple times beginning with incandescent light bulbs before becoming neon lights, LEDs
and today the whole set of advertising signs are actually just one bright display with over 11.8
million pixels – it was upgraded in 2017.

"Circus" in Piccadilly Circus' name is Latin for circle, as this is a major road junction – the
Shaftesbury Memorial Fountain, now in a pedestrianised area, was the centre of a roundabout
until after WWII. The memorial dates from 1893 and remembers Lord Shaftesbury, a philanthropist and politician who amongst other things is remembered for making sure young boys
were not used as chimney sweeps due to the health implications. Many Londoners call it the
statue on top 'Eros' (the Greek God of Love) but it is in fact 'Anteros' (symbolising Shaftesbury's selfless love).

Also on Piccadilly Circus is the entry to the Criterion Theatre, a 600-seat West End theatre
which is almost entirely underground. Lillywhites next door is a sporting goods store which
has stood on this site since 1925 – today it is owned by a major chain, Sports Direct, and we
feel it is has long lost much of its charm and cachet, and feels like any other chain sports shop.

Head up Shaftesbury Avenue, named after the aforementioned Lord Shaftesbury until you reach Macclesfield
Street on the right. As you can tell from the signs and
décor, you are now in Chinatown (14).

London's current Chinatown is a relatively new part of the
city, starting its life in the 1970s – it was previously based
in East London since the early 20th century. Compared to
many other world cities, particularly in the USA, London's
Chinatown is relatively small consisting on only a handful of
streets.

Turn right onto Wardour Street.

On the right at number 41-43 Wardour Street, just ahead is
Wong Kei's (15) – one of the UK's largest Chinese restaurants with seating for 500 people – the restaurant rose to
fame for its bad customer service and was described in the
Guardian as "the rudest restaurant in London".

Complaints included diners being separated onto different tables, chased out the building for not tipping enough,
shouted at and mocked for asking for a knife and fork, and
even accused of lying if anything was found in their food.
It has operated under new management since 2014 and the
new waiters are noticeably less rude.

Continue up Wardour Street onto Whitcomb Street and ahead to the corner with M&Ms
World on Panton street. Turn left onto Swiss Court.

Here you will see in the middle of the walkway a clock surrounded by bells in a Swiss theme.
This is the Swiss Glockenspiel (16) which has stood here since 2011. However, its history dates
back much further than 2011. The Glockenspiel used to be part of the façade of the Swiss Cen-

tre which stood where M&Ms world is today. The Swiss Centre was a tourist attraction themed around Switzerland with Swiss-themed restaurants, shops, a bank, a tourism office and more. The original glockenspiel was a gift of friendship from Switzerland and Liechtenstein in 1984. The newly redesigned musical clock features 27 bells which ring on the hour along with 11 moving figures which rotate around the podium. A few metres away, is a flagpole with the Confederation's 26 state flags, which also used to stand on the Swiss Centre.

Continue ahead into Leicester Square (17). **On this tour we will stay on this (north) side of the square straight ahead of you, though do feel free to explore areas of the square before re-joining the route.**

Leicester Square (pronounced lester) is named after Leicester House which used to stand on the site of the square in the 1630s, owned by Robert Sidney, 2nd Earl of Leicester. Before that this land was part of the Abbot and Convent of Westminster Abbey until it was seized by Henry VIII in 1536.

The West End has a long history of being involved with arts as, by the 19th century, it was already a famed entertainment spot including many theatres which still stand today. In the middle of the square is a garden upon which is a statue of Shakespeare with a fountain around it, the statue dating from 1874. There is also a statue of Charlie Chaplin on the square added in 1981. Across the square is a small building with a clock on top: this is TKTS, the official discount theatre booth, which offers genuine bargains on many shows.

Leicester Square is perhaps most famous today for its film premieres. With several major cinemas flanking the square (Odeon, Vue and Cineworld), the red carpet is out most weeks welcoming stars and fans, mainly outside Odeon.

Continue through Leicester Square ahead, passing Burger King on your right until you reach the busy Charing Cross Road.

On the corner on the left is The Hippodrome (18), an enormous casino today with space for 2000 guests at the same time. It began its life in 1900 as a venue for circus performances and, at one point, enormous aquatic spectacles where the stage sank into a tank. It has also served as a theatre and a nightclub in its time.

Cross over using the pedestrian crossing outside Leicester Square station, turn right on Charing Cross Road and head down Cecil Court (19) **shortly on the left.**

Cecil Court often feels a world away from the busy areas of Leicester Square and Piccadilly Circus. Harry Potter fans will likely instantly recognise the street as it is widely believed to have been one of two streets in this area that formed the inspiration for Diagon Alley in the Harry Potter books and films. Cecil Court is indeed filled with unique booksellers, antique shops and map sellers. The current buildings were laid out in the 1890s. Cecil Court was also instrumental in the beginning of the British film industry and has gained it the nickname "Flicker Alley".

The street also has musical history: Number 9 has a blue plaque as a reminder that composer Mozart lived here at the age of 8 years old while he was touring Europe in 1764. Mozart and his family lodged with barber John Couzin for almost 4 months. Tickets for his first London concerts were sold at Couzin's shop. Mozart also performed on two occasions for King George III while living at number 9. Once out the other side of Cecil's Court you are on St. Martin's Lane.

Cross the street and on the left look out for the easy-to-miss entrance to Goodwin's Court almost immediately on the right. If you make it to New Row, you have gone too far. Head inside Goodwin's Court (20).

Goodwin's Court is said to have been another one of the inspirations for Diagon Alley, particularly the Georgian bowed display windows. There are still working gas lamps along the passage. A plaque on site details that "it seems probable" the current buildings were erected in 1690.

Turn left at the end, then right onto New Row. Cross over Bedford Street onto King Street.

The first building on the left with the Prince of Wales feathers and crests on the façade was home to the fire office from the 1850s until 1906.

Continue along King Street to the corner of Covent Garden's main piazza, with St. Paul's Church (21) **on your right.**

St. Paul's Church is known as the "actor's church" and dates from 1633. It was designed by Inigo Jones as well as much of the original square and houses which stood in the area. It was the first completely new church to be built since the Reformation of the 1530s.

Opposite the church in the centre of the piazza is the Punch and Judy pub. Covent Garden was where Samuel Pepys recorded the first instance of a Punch and Judy show in Britain performed by an Italian performer. For those unfamiliar with Punch and Judy, these shows are often played at seaside venues for the entertainment of the whole family. The story often revolved around Punch (the dad), who is often tasked with looking after his baby by Judy (the wife) – after failing to do so, the duo end up hitting each other with sticks in a farcical way as the audience cheer them on.

Covent Garden's (22) **dates back to the thirteenth century when it was part of Westminster Abbey's Convent Garden.**

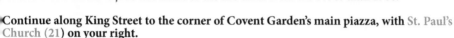

In 1552, the land was seized from the church by Henry VIII and granted to the Earls of Bedford who developed it into a wealthy neighbourhood with a large square at its centre. By the mid-seventeenth century, the square was a fashionable place to be seen and held an open-air fruit and vegetable market, though the area then fell into disrepute and became a red-light district. The current covered structure, by Charles Fowler, in the middle of the square dates from 1830 and by the early 1900s the market had expanded to include flowers and other produce, as well as fruit and vegetables. Today this building is an upmarket shopping and dining area, so do feel free to explore it. It is especially beautiful at Christmas.

Continue around the outside of the central covered buildings clockwise, heading past the Jubilee Market (today used to sell souvenirs) towards the London Transport Museum (23).

The building occupied by the museum was the former home of the flower market in Covent Garden, until 1971. The museum moved in in 1980 and provides a fascinating insight into the importance of transport for London.

Continue clockwise. Turn right down Russell Street

In the distance is the Theatre Royal Drury Lane (24), the oldest theatre site in London which has been in continuous use since 1663 – the current building dates from 1812.

Turn left down Bow Street. Continue until the Royal Opera House (25) **on the left.**

The towering ROH is the home of The Royal Opera, The Royal Ballet, and the Orchestra of the Royal Opera House. The current building dates from 1858, though an extensive refurbishment in the 1990s replaced much of the aging theatre. The Royal Opera House's roots date back to 1662 when its precursor was founded as the Theatre Royal, Covent Garden. The building seats 2,256 people, making it the third largest auditorium in London.

Continue down Bow Street onto Endell Street. Turn left onto Shorts Gardens.

Further down, look for Holland and Barrett on the right. Here, look up for the unique Neal's Yard Water Clock (26).

The clock was created in 1982 and no longer works in the way it should. Originally, on the hour, a tank on the roof of the building would empty causing water to tip through a variety of funnels with bells attached to create a melody. When the water reached the bottom it would end up at one of the figures holding watering cans; the figures would then tip the water into a box behind the shopfront's sign and this would cause flowers to float up, giving the appearance of them growing. The figure on the far left, however, tipped water onto unsuspecting passers-by. Under the clock is a pipe which would fill up throughout the hour to display the time.

26

To the left of Holland and Barrett is a barrel marking the entrance to Neal's Yard (27). Head down this alley.

Neal's Yard is a small, colourful courtyard unlike anywhere else in London. The area gets its name from Thomas Neale, a 17th-century developer. This is the home of health foods, organic products and socially conscious enterprises in London with several different eateries and cafes to try. We highly recommend Homeslice Pizza (walk-ins only or call ahead for collection). Veggie and vegans will love Wild Food Café, and Native is a great all-round restaurant.

27

Above Neal's Yard Remedies, look for a blue plaque to Monty Python, where the comedy group's offices were based and where the films were edited from.

Head out of Neal's Yard to the left of Neal's Yard Remedies onto Monmouth Street. Turn left. You soon reach a monument in the centre of the road – Seven Dials (28).

Seven Dials was developed by the aforementioned Thomas Neale and the original layout was dates from the 17th century. The original plans called for only six roads converging at this one spot hence why the column in the middle (which is actually a sundial) only has six faces.

28

This street layout enabled the landowners to make more money, as the plots of land around this area would all be triangular in shape allowing for more metres of house fronts when rents were charged by the width and height of facades.

Despite Neale's intentions of creating a wealthy area, Seven Dials became one of London's worst slums in the Victorian era and was synonymous with chronic overcrowding. Today the area is characterised by its upmarket shops. The column in the centre still acts as a sundial, though it is a replica from 1989 and not the original one.

Head west down Earlham Street (opposite the Cambridge Theatre). Turn left on Shaftesbury Avenue and then right onto Charing Cross Road.

Follow the road, passing Foyles (29) on your left – once, Foyles was the Guinness World Record Holder of the world's largest bookshop in terms of shelf length, at 30 miles (48 km), as well as the number of titles on display.

Walk up the road to Tottenham Court Road station where this tour ends.

Walk 5: South Bank and Along the Thames

Walk Length: 3.60 km / 2.23 mi
Timings: 1h 45m (fast), 2h (regular), 2h 15m (leisurely)
Start: Westminster station
End: Westminster station

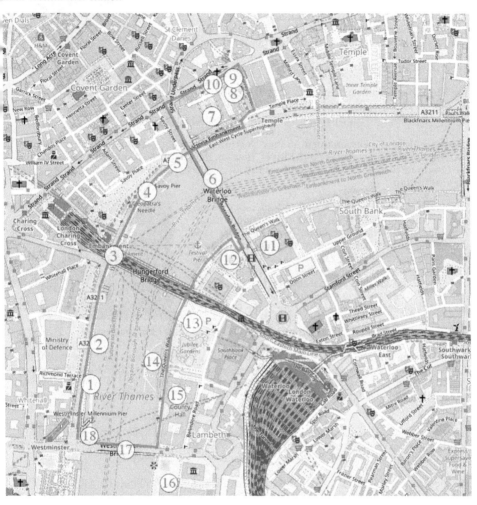

(1) Battle of Britain Memorial	(10) King's College
(2) Royal Air Force Memorial	(11) Royal National Theatre
(3) Hungerford Bridge	(12) Royal Festival Hall
(4) Cleopatra's Needle	(13) Shell Tower
(5) Red Telephone Box	(14) London Eye
(6) Waterloo Bridge	(15) County Hall
(7) Somerset House	(16) St. Thomas' Hospital
(8) Roman Bath	(17) Westminster Bridge
(9) Aldwych Station	(18) Queen Boudicca Statue

Begin at Westminster Station. Use Exit 1 for Westminster Pier. This tour does not cover the Parliament Square and Big Ben area – for this, see walk 3. When at Exit 1 and near the pier, turn left and walk approx. 200m until you arrive at the Battle of Britain Memorial (1).

The often-missed Battle of Britain memorial remembers the 1940 battle as part of WWII in which Britain's Royal Air Force defended the UK against attacks from the German Luftwaffe. The battle lasted 3 months and 3 days from 10 July to 31 October 1940, and overlaps with the period known as The Blitz in which the UK was bombed by aerial attacks at night.

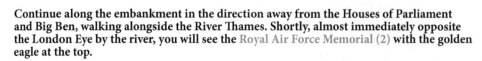

The height of the battle is remembered as Battle of Britain Day on 15 September 1940 in which 1,500 aircraft bombed London and the English Channel throughout the day and evening.

Continue along the embankment in the direction away from the Houses of Parliament and Big Ben, walking alongside the River Thames. Shortly, almost immediately opposite the London Eye by the river, you will see the Royal Air Force Memorial (2) with the golden eagle at the top.

The memorial was unveiled in 1923 in remembrance of the members of the Royal Air Force who fought during WWI and all subsequent conflicts. The memorial is opposite the Ministry of Defence across the road. The eagle at the top is a reference to the eagle on the RAF badge and faces south towards France; it stands atop a globe. There are inscriptions on the memorial relating to both WWI and WWII. The RAF motto "Per ardua ad astra" is also inscribed, meaning "Through Adversity to the Stars".

Now look at the black dolphin lampposts by the river along the embankment.

The base of the lamp posts is based on statues of dolphins from the Fontana del Nettuno in Rome, with these lampposts being designed by George John Vulliamy in 1870. Vulliamy was, at the time, the superintending architect to the Metropolitan Board of Works. A little known fact is that although the lamps have been nicknamed "dolphin lamps", the fish depicted are actual sturgeons.

The Victoria Embankment that you are working along is an important thoroughfare for Londoners today but this vital piece of infrastructure was only constructed between 1865 and 1870 under the direction of famed Victorian civil engineer Joseph Bazalgette.

The Victoria Embankment runs from the Palace of Westminster to Blackfriars Bridge, and is accompanied by two other embankments on the other side of the Palace of Westminster – the Albert Embankment and the Chelsea Embankment.

The enormous embankment project was spurred by the need for a modern sewerage system. Until the embankments were built, the River Thames was an open sewer with sewage flowing along the streets into the river. The city was rife with disease (cholera in particular) and despite numerous proposals for a new sewer, it was only in 1858 that the issue was taken seriously after an incident termed the "Great Stink" in which the heat made the smell so unbearable that parliament took notice as their newly rebuilt parliament building standing right next to the river.

The Victoria Embankment was a step change for London,

including a sewer, a cut-and-cover tunnel for the District Railway and a major road on top (relieving congestion on Fleet Street and Strand), as well as new public gardens. The 5-year project narrowed the River Thames significantly and necessitated the purchase of expensive riverside property.

Today, the Victorian sewerage system is inadequate for London's growing population and, on average, once a week sewage pollutes the Thames. A 25km "supersewer" is under construction as part of the Thames Tideway scheme with a target completion date of 2023 at a construction cost of £4.2 billion in its 2012 estimate.

Continue along the embankment until you reach the Hungerford Bridge (3).
The original bridge was designed by Isambard Kingdom Brunel as a suspension footbridge, though the current bridge (exclusively used by the railways) dates from 1864 and was designed by John Hawkshaw. The original redbrick supports from Brunel's bridge can be seen in the Thames by the embankment.

Today the Hungerford Bridge is partially obscured by the white footbridges running along both sides. The Golden Jubilee Bridges opened in 2002 to celebrate the 50th anniversary of Queen Elizabeth II's coronation.

Head under the bridge ahead along the embankment, passing Embankment Pier .

Running alongside you is the East-West Cycle Superhighway – an 18-mile, £47 million investment in cycling infrastructure completed in phases between 2015 and 2018.

Shortly, you reach Cleopatra's Needle (4) **on your right.**

Cleopatra's Needle is often regarded as London's oldest outdoor monument dating back to 1450 BC. The obelisk is one of three: the two others are in New York City and Paris. With the London and NYC one being part of a pair. The name is a misnomer as the needle has nothing to do with Queen Cleopatra who came almost 1500 years later; the needle was originally sited in the Egyptian city of Heliopolis under instructions of Pharoah Thutmose III. It was presented to the UK by the Egyptian ruler Mohammed Ali in 1819 to commemorate the victories at the Battle of the Nile (1798) and Battle of Alexandria (1801). It was eventually erected in 1877 after being transported by sea.

The sphinxes guarding the needle are curiously facing the wrong way; they should be facing outwards to "guard" the needle. It is claimed they were placed facing the needle as Queen Victoria preferred the look of this.

4

The right hand side of the obelisk as well as the base of the right-hand sphinx has significant shrapnel damage as a bomb was dropped nearby during WWII.

Continue alongside the Embankment ahead.

Note the frequent benches here; these were designed by Vulliamy who also designed the dolphin lamps and the sphinxes by Cleopatra's Needle. In preparation for the Needle's installation, benches in the area were given an extra ornate touch. Look out for one of these just before or after the Needle with the armrests designed as sphinxes. Many of the benches were refurbished in the 1970s.

Stop before you reach Waterloo Bridge by the red telephone box (5).

These famed red telephone boxes are a common sight throughout central London, particularly in Westminster. The boxes were designed by Sir Giles Gilbert Scott and there have been 8 different designs over the years. Differences in models include size, panelling, materials and even the crown at the top – the most popular design is the K6 dating from 1935.

The arch at the top of the phone box creating the roof is said to have inspired the arches of Waterloo Bridge ahead, both designed by the Scott.

Waterloo Bridge (6) commemorates the British, Dutch and Prussian victory at the Battle of Waterloo against the French in 1815. The bridge was constructed during WWII, largely by women, and is therefore nicknamed the "ladies' bridge" – it opened in 1942. Crossing the bridge offers some of the best views of London's skyline, and you will be doing so shortly.

Continue under Waterloo Bridge until you reach the Royal National Lifeboat Institution Station on the Thames. Look across the road for the magnificent arches of Somerset House (7).

The road running parallel to the Victoria Embankment, behind Somerset House, is called Strand and was in the 16th century a very desirable location for palaces, which would overlook the River Thames; the site of Somerset House was no exception to this. In 1549, Edward Seymour (Duke of Somerset) began construction of his residence (Old Somerset House) on this site – a two-storey house around a quadrangle with the outer wall touching the river Thames. The house was demolished in 1775, after decades of neglect.

The current Somerset House was designed by William Chambers and construction started immediately upon the demolition of the old building. The new building was not to be a palace, but a location for many government offices, notably The Admiralty. In the 18th century, the archways on the building façade on the embankment would have touched the river, and boats would have entered through some of these arches to dock.

Today the building is mainly used for events such as London Fashion Week, as well as being the home of the Courtauld Gallery (mostly French Impressionist paintings) and other galleries. It also hosts a wonderful Christmas event with an ice rink in the colder months.

After walking past Somerset House, cross the street and head down Temple Place. Note the statue of Isambard Kingdom Brunel, the famed architect from earlier in the tour. Turn left onto Temple Place, then left down narrow Strand Lane. [If the gate to this street is closed, head onto Surrey Street and continue the tour from the next section].

If the gate is open, followed the dotted line on our map until you pass some steps on your right and see a plaque for the Roman Baths. If the gate is closed follow the maps' solid line.

The building ahead with the alleyway continuing under it and the ironworks around the windows on the first floor is the Old Watch House for the parishes of St. Clement Dane and St. Mary-Le-Strand. This street is actually the boundary between the two parishes. This building is where watchmen or "Charlies" (security personnel) would gather before their nightly patrols.

The brick building to its right with the plaque on the gates is the Roman Baths (8). The name is a misnomer as these are neither baths nor roman. The remains are in fact thought to be part of a cistern for a fountain in the old Somerset House gardens, at the time a royal palace. They were used as a public cold plunge bath in the 1770s and the Roman identity was likely an advertising gimmick.

Retrace your steps slightly until you come to the Surrey Steps. Go up these steps, emerging onto Surrey Street. If the gates for these steps are closed return back onto Temple Place, turn left and left again onto Surrey Street.

Turn left and walk up Surrey Street until you reach a red-tiled building on your left with "Piccadilly Railway" and "Exit" and "Entrance" signs. This is the former Aldwych Station (9).

8

Aldwych Station is one of many abandoned Underground Stations which are no longer in regular use today; it was originally called Strand station when it opened in 1907. The ox-blood red-tiling style was popularised by architect Leslie Green and was used in over 50 stations across the city.

The station was served by the Piccadilly Railway and was a short branch line from Holborn station – the two stations are a mere 10-minute walk from each other. Service was gradually reduced from 1962 to weekday peak hours only and then the branch and the station were shut altogether in 1994 due to low passenger numbers and the prohibitive expense of replacing the lifts.

9

The station is today often used for filming and it was also used to keep artworks from galleries and museums safe during WWII. Filming with moving trains in the station may become impossible in the future as the tunnel used to link the station to Holborn station will be used as part of a redevelopment of Holborn station in the early 2020s. Aldwych Station is currently occasionally opened for guided tours.

Continue up Surrey Street, turning left onto Strand. Walk past the other entrance to Strand/Aldwych Station until you are level with King's College (10) **on the left and St. Mary Le Strand Church (dating from 1723) on the right.**

King's College is one of London's premiere learning institutions, having been established in 1829. The university has five campuses and was ranked 23rd in the 2018 QS World University Rankings. Notable alumni include Nobel Prize winners Peter Higgs (theorist of the Higgs boson particle), poet John Keats, writer Virginia Woolf and Bentley Motors founder Walter Bentley.

Continue past the arches of Somerset House (7).

Do take a detour inside if you wish, and see the magnificent courtyard (you may recognise it as the Ministry of Defence in James Bond's Tomorrow Never Dies).

7

Two doors further down is Gibraltar House, where the diplomatic mission of the British Overseas Territory of Gibraltar is based.

Continue to the major junction with Lancaster Place. Cross the road and turn left along Lancaster Place onto Waterloo Bridge. Cross Waterloo Bridge (6) **over the River Thames.**

Due to its unique location on the bend of the River Thames, Waterloo Bridge affords some of the best views of London's skyline with the Houses of Parliament and the London Eye in the City of Westminster to the right, and the financial district's skyscrapers and St. Paul's Cathedral to the left in the City of London.

Beneath is the River Thames, this section of which is tidal, rising and falling by 23 feet (7m). It is the second-longest river in the UK after the River Severn, and is 215 miles (346 km) long. Today, the River Thames could cause floods in London were it not for the Thames Barrier in east London, which controls the amount of water in the river's central section. Since its opening in 1984, the Thames Barrier has been used 179 times up to October 2017.

Joseph Bazalgette's sewer system (discussed earlier in this walk), along with strong government policy to deter factories from dumping in the river, has gained the Thames the moniker of the cleanest river in the world to flow through any major city. The brown-ish colour is the Thames is due to the sediment moving with the tide.

Although it is almost impossible to imagine it today, the River Thames historically froze over – a total of at least 24 times from the 15th century to the 19th century. London's weather was more extreme, the river was wider and slower moving, and the archways of the old London bridge severely impeded the movement of water. At times the ice was so thick that frost fairs took place – the greatest of these was in the winter of 1683-84 in which the ice was 11 inches thick and the river froze over for two months. During frost fairs, people played football on the ice, puppet shows took place, the monarchs rode on sleighs, and in 1814 an elephant was even led across the river!

Cross Waterloo Bridge until you reach The Southbank, known for its cultural venues.

Look left at the concrete building on the other side of the road – this is the Brutalist-style Royal National Theatre (11), dating from 1976. There are varied performances inside, usually at affordable prices. To the right is Royal Festival Hall (12).

Follow the path down the steps to the right where the white railing ends until you are at ground level.

12

Royal Festival Hall is the only surviving building of the 1951 Festival of Britain. This was the centenary year of the 1851 Great Exhibition (the first world's fair) held in Hyde Park. The 1951 festival focused on Britain and its achievements – a way of uniting the nation after WWII.

Today, Royal Festival Hall is one of several buildings which are part of the Southbank Centre, comprising a 2500-seat live performance venue and the Hayward Gallery. The "Undercroft" of the Southbank Centre at ground level houses the somewhat grotty-looking Southbank skatepark which often features in music videos. In 2014, the skatepark was saved from demolition after a long campaign to save it.

Underneath Waterloo Bridge you will find the British Film Institute (BFI). This includes a four-screen cinema venue showing over 2,000 classic and contemporary films each year, with film seasons, director and actor retrospectives, and extended runs of cinema classics. You can view over 1000 hours of free film and TV in the Mediatheque, visit the library and film shop, and enjoy two restaurant bars. The BFI National Archive, the largest film archive in the world contains 150,000 movies and around 625,000 television programs. There is also often a book market under Waterloo Bridge.

Continue past Royal Festival Hall, under the Hungerford Bridge, to the London Eye.

Before reaching the London Eye, almost immediately level with it to the left stands a tall building adorning flagpoles at the top. This is the 351-foot-tall [107 m] Shell Tower (13), one of the global headquarters of oil giant Shell. The tower was the first London office tower to exceed the height of the Victoria Tower of the Palace of Westminster. It was completed in 1962.

Today the site is home to a £1.3 billion "Southbank Place" redevelopment which will include seven new blocks around the Shell Tower with offices, 868 homes (of which a mere 98 will be deemed "affordable"), shops and dining locations due for completion in 2019.

Now turn your attention to the London Eye (14)**.**

The London Eye was originally called the Millennium Wheel and was supposed to be a temporary addition for the year 2000 that would only stay for up to five years. Standing at 443 feet (135 m) tall, this was the tallest Ferris wheel in the world when it opened. To this day, it is still the tallest cantilevered (supports on one side only) observation wheel in the world.

Construction of the London Eye was an enormous project and took place on the River Thames by barges as different parts of the structure came from different European countries; in late 1999, the wheel was tilted into place over the course of several weeks.

14

A ride on the London Eye take 30 minutes (passengers board as the wheel moves), and each pod has room for 25 guests. There are 32 pods, supposedly one for each London borough. It is the most popular paid attraction in the UK, with 3.75 million visitors yearly and is now one the most recognisable landmarks on the city's skyline, along with Big Ben and St. Paul's.

Continue past the London Eye alongside the river until you are level with County Hall (15) **on the left, which houses the London Eye ticket office.**

15

County Hall was the former home of London's government between 1922 and 1986. The building dates from 1922. Today it functions as a hotel, and contains an arcade, the London Dungeon, Shrek's Adventure and an aquarium. London's government is today run from City Hall by Tower Bridge.

Continue up the steps towards St. Thomas' Hospital (16) **opposite.**

St. Thomas' Hospital is named after Thomas Beckett, Archbishop of Canterbury from 1162 to 1170. Beckett publicly disagreed with King Henry II over the rights of the Church and was murdered by followers of the King in Canterbury Cathedral. He is remembered as a martyr and was canonised as a saint.

The hospital is home to the pioneering Florence Nightingale Faculty of Nursing and Midwifery, established in 1860 by Florence Nightingale. There is a museum dedicated to Nightingale, the founder of modern nursing, inside.

Turn right. Walk across Westminster Bridge (17) **with an excellent view of the Houses of Parliament, also known as the Palace of Westminster.**

Today's Westminster Bridge dates from 1862, though the previous bridge stood on this site since 1750. Until this year, London Bridge further east was the only bridge in central London. When there was only one bridge, traffic from the West End going to south London had to detour along Strand and Fleet Street and across London Bridge, causing congestion in the city.

Today's bridge stands 820 feet (250 m) long and was designed by Thomas Page. The Gothic detailing is the work of Charles Barry, who was also the architect of the Palace of Westminster.

Across the bridge, to the right, is a statue of Queen Boudicca (18). Boudicca was queen of the Iceni tribe, who led an unsuccessful revolt of 100,000 Celts against the Romans in AD60-61. During her uprising, she burnt London to the ground. Boudicca died shortly after the rebellion.

Here ends the tour. Take the steps down to the pier for Westminster Station.

Walk 6: Hyde Park and Kensington Gardens Walk
Walk Length: 5.10 km / 3.17 mi
Timings: 2h (fast), 2h 30m (regular), 3h (leisurely)
Start: Marble Arch station
End: Queensway station

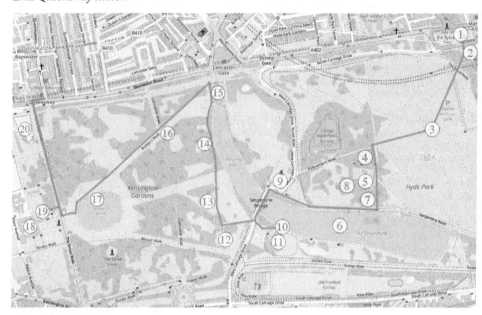

(1) Marble Arch
(2) Speakers' Corner
(3) Reformers' Tree
(4) Old Police House
(5) Rangers Lodge
(6) The Serpentine
(7) Royal Humane Society
(8) Norwegian War Memorial
(9) Serpentine Sackler Gallery
(10) Isis Sculpture

(11) Diana Memorial Fountain
(12) Serpentine Gallery
(13) Queen Caroline's Temple
(14) Statue of Peter Pan
(15) Italian Water Gardens
(16) Speke Monument
(17) Round Pond
(18) Kensington Palace
(19) Sunken Garden
(20) Diana Memorial Playground

A note about this walk:
This tour is slightly different to our other tours as it takes place almost entirely inside Hyde Park and Kensington Gardens. The pathways in the park do not have distinct names like roads, so please use the map to follow the tour carefully it is easy to take a wrong turn. It is also worth checking the opening hours of both parks online before embarking on this tour; Hyde Park closes at midnight and Kensington Gardens shuts at sunset.

This tour begins at Marble Arch Station. Use the exit signposted for Hyde Park and Marble Arch. You will emerge at ground level near Marble Arch (1) **itself.**

Before this area was known as Marble Arch, it was called Tyburn named after the Tyburn Brook which now flows underground. Tyburn was just outside London and was most famous for being the place of public executions. Hangings took place off gallows called the Tyburn Tree - up to 24 people could be hanged at once. Notably hanged here was Jack Sheppard, a thief, whose execution attracted 200,000 spectators in 1724 – about a third of London's population.

1

Hangings were often public holidays and were incredibly popular. Prisoners were brought down from Newgate Prison – a distance of three miles. The ill-fated were usually allowed to stop for one last drink at a pub along the way, thought to be the origin of the phrase "one for the road"; the drivers of the wagons which transported them were not allowed to drink, giving us the expression of being "on the wagon".

Today, Tyburn is simply referred as Marble Arch thanks to the marble archway moved here in 1851. The archway, designed by John Nash in 1827, was previously outside Buckingham Palace and was its grand entranceway. However, in the 1840s, the palace was deemed to small and by 1847 the arch had been dismantled. It was rebuilt on its current site a few years later.

Use the pedestrian crossings to reach Hyde Park and enter through the gates on the park's corner. You are now in an area known as Speakers' Corner (2).

Speakers' Corner is the north-east corner of Hyde Park. Here on Sunday mornings you can take in one of London's finest free spectacles as people take a soapbox, stand on it and exercise their right of free speech. Anyone can take part in spectating or speaking.

The origins of the practice stem back to 1866 in which a meeting of the Reform League, demanding the extension of the right to vote to all men, was suppressed by the Government. Finding the park locked, demonstrators tore up hundreds of yards of railings to enter, and three days of rioting followed. The next year, 150,000 protesters defied another government ban and marched to Hyde Park; this time the police did not intervene. In 1872, the Parks Regulation Act established the right to meet and speak freely in Hyde Park. The tradition continues to this day as large protests often begin here at Speakers' Corner before marching to Parliament Square.

Follow the map taking the path in a south-westerly direction towards the tall tower in the distance. If you see in-park signs, follow those pointing to The Serpentine. After about 300m you will reach a mosaic of the Reformers' Tree (3) **on the ground.**

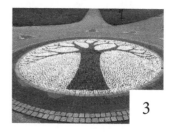

3

The original Reformers' Tree was a real tree. In 1866, The Reform League, mentioned at Speakers' Corner, burnt the oak tree which stood on this site as part as one of their protests, using the stump as a podium and meeting point. The tree is today remembered by the mosaic, which was unveiled in 2000.

Around the mosaic are arrows pointing to various areas of the park. Take the path signposted "Kensington Gardens / The Old Police House" for about 250m to the red-brick Old Police House. Take a left to walk along the front.

The Old Police House (4) is today the main office of The Royal Parks, the charity that manages eight royal parks in London totalling over 5,000 acres. The main funding for the parks is a grant from central government; other income is generated through commercial activities such as the park's cafes and staging public events such as concerts. The Old Police House building dates from 1902 and is on the site of previous police accommodation. To the left of this grand building stands the modest Rangers Lodge (5), dating from 1832.

Continue down the path past Rangers Lodge until you reach The Serpentine Lake (6).

To understand Hyde Park better, it is worth understand how the park came to be. The park was originally the property of Westminster Abbey, but was seized by Henry VIII in 1536 and became his hunting ground – at the time it was filled with wild deer. In 1637, Charles I opened the park to the public, and it immediately became popular.

In 1730, Queen Caroline (wife of King George II) ordered a lake be built in the park – today's Serpentine. The lake's name is supposedly due to its shape, looking like a snake from above – the lake was one of the first in the city to take on a natural design, as most man-made lakes at the time were of a fixed rectangular-like shape.

Today, The Serpentine is mainly used for recreational purposes. You can hire paddle boats, and in the summer a solar-powered boat also runs along the lake. There is even a year-round outdoor swimming lido. The lake was even used during the 2012 Olympic Games for the swimming portion of triathlon events.

Take a look back at the path you just came from. To the left is a small house under the trees. This small building is the home of the Royal Humane Society (7), founded in 1774 to help in cases of near drowning in the park - at the time most people could not swim but many would enter lakes, such as The Serpentine for recreation purposes.

Continue westwards alongside The Serpentine. At the second small boathouse along the lake, look to the right across the grass at a large rock in the distance.

This boulder is the, somewhat understated, Norwegian War Memorial (8). It was presented by the Norwegian Navy and Merchant Fleet to the British in 1978 for the country's support during WWII. The granite boulder stands on three smaller stones and features inscriptions.

Continue along the lake, to the right through a car park to a major road and the Serpentine Sackler Gallery (9) **across the road on the right. If you are walking under a bridge, retrace your steps to get onto the bridge itself.**

The Serpentine Sackler Gallery's main building was originally a munitions depot dating from 1805. It also contains a modern extension from Zara Hadid Architects added in 2013. It holds art and architecture exhibitions. Admission is free and the gallery is open from 10:00am to 6:00pm from Tuesday to Sunday, plus bank holidays. It is closed on Mondays.

Follow the road, cross the bridge to the other side of The Serpentine and take the first path to the left. Follow the path towards the lake until you reach a statue of a bird.

This bird is Isis (10), the name of an Egyptian goddess. The statue was unveiled in 2009 and was designed by Simon Gudgeon. The 633kg bronze sculpture contains a coin hole and its aim was to raise £1.8m for an environmental education centre; the centre ('The LookOut') was fully funded by 2011 and donations now help to continue running both the centre and the Royal Parks.

The centrepiece of this area is the Diana Memorial Fountain (11). Unveiled in 2004 by Queen Elizabeth II, the fountain is made of Cornish Granite and is a place to reflect on the life of Diana, Princess of Wales who lived in nearby Kensington Palace (seen later in the walk).

The design of the memorial supposedly reflects Diana's life as "water flows... in two directions as it cascades, swirls and bubbles before meeting in a calm pool at the bottom… The Memorial also symbolises Diana's quality and openness. There are three bridges where you can cross the water and go right to the heart of the fountain."

During cold or severe weather, the water may be turned off or access to the memorial closed. It is scheduled to open daily from 10:00am – closing times vary seasonally from 4:00pm to 8:00pm.

Retrace your steps back to the main road by the bridge. This is West Carriage Drive, which separates Hyde Park from Kensington Gardens. Cross the road to Kensington Gardens. Take the middle path ahead travelling in a Westerly direction. After 150m is an area with many paths. To the left is the Serpentine Gallery (12).

The Serpentine Gallery was founded in 1970, and is housed in a former tea pavilion dating from 1934 by the architect James Grey West. Like the Serpentine Sackler Gallery seen earlier, admission is free. In the summer, you may notice the temporary summer pavilion, usually a more modern, structure next to the Serpentine Gallery. Each year an international architect or design team who has not completed a building in England is chosen to design the pavilion. Each Pavilion is situated on the Gallery's lawn for three months for the public to explore and is completed in under six months.

Take the path to the right in the direction northwards, opposite to the gallery, and you very quickly reach Queen Caroline's Temple (13) **on your left.**

13

Queen Caroline, who we discussed earlier, wanted the addition of The Serpentine in Hyde Park. Another request was a summer house, today called Queen Caroline's Temple, built in 1734-35 in a classical style and designed by William Kent. The building was converted to a parkkeeper's home later in its life, but it was restored to its use as a summer house in 1976.

Continue along the path to the lake, called The Long Water. Follow the path by the water's edge northwards (to the left). Soon you reach an open section with a railing looking over the water and two benches – to the left here is a gate leading to a statue of Peter Pan (14).

14

Peter Pan was far from a Disney creation; the 'boy who wouldn't grow up' was a figment of J. M. Barrie's imagination. Barrie was a local resident and was said to be inspired by Kensington Gardens. Barrie commissioned this statue in 1912 and it was designed by Sir George Frampton. Barrie gave the copyright if the Peter Pan character to Great Ormond Street Hospital for Children in London, which still benefits from royalty payments when the characters are used.

Continue north on the path to the Italian Water Gardens (15).

15

The Italian Gardens' inspiration can be traced to Osborne House on The Isle of Wight, where the royal family spent their holidays. Here, Prince Albert took care of the gardens and introduced an Italian garden with large raised terraces, fountains, urns and geometric flower beds. In 1860, he brought this design to Kensington Gardens as a gift to Queen Victoria.

There are five main urn designs to look out for: a swan's breast, woman's head, ram's head, dolphin and oval. The small building at the end is called the Pump House and originally contained a steam engine which operated the fountains – note the chimney. Overlooking the gardens on the Eastern side is a statue of Edward Jenner, who invented the smallpox vaccine. The statue was originally in Trafalgar Square but was moved here in 1862.

Follow the map in a south-westerly direction. After about 300m you will see the Speke Monument (16) **on your left.**

John Hanning Speke was an explorer who led expeditions to the source of the River Nile. Speke claimed the source was the Rippon Falls, an outflow from Lake Victoria in east Africa; when Speke was proven correct, the Royal Geographical Society said he had solved "the problem of all ages". The obelisk memorial dates from 1866 and was designed by Philip Hardwick.

Continue south-westerly, ignoring the paths that cross your route until you reach the Round Pond (17), **about 400m after the Speke Monument.**

Kensington Gardens was part of the original land which Henry VIII seized and formed part of Hyde Park on. In 1728, Queen Caroline (King George II's wife) requested that this parcel land be separated and Kensington Gardens was born – a private garden for Kensington Palace. Tree-lined avenues with created to form a landscaped garden, and other fashionable features such as the Round Pound were added. The Round Pond was created under the request of George II and was completed in 1730. It is 16 ft (5m) deep and covers 7 acres.

Follow the path around the pond to Kensington Palace (18). **At the entrance is a white statue of Queen Victoria, who grew up at this palace. The road across the front is Broad Walk.**

Kensington Palace was originally a two-storey mansion built in 1605 in the village of Kensington. In 1689, King William I and Queen Mary II (joint monarchs) bought the house as William suffered from asthma and needed cleaner air than he had available at the Palace of Whitehall which stood next to the dirty River Thames.

Famed architect Christopher Wren began immediate work on expanding the property. The palace became the home of the British Monarch for next seventy years. In the reign of Queen Anne in 1702, the Queen's apartments were added. George I had significant expansions added creating the King's apartments, whereas George II allowed his wife Caroline to run the palace – no major additions to the palace were made, but the gardens were completely remodelled.

More recently, the palace was home to Prince Charles and Diana, Princess of Wales from 1981 until Diana's death in 1997 (including after the couple's divorce). William and Harry were raised here. Today, Prince William and Kate Middleton live here with their children. Prince Harry also lives here, and Megan Markle is due to move in after the couple's wedding in 2018.

Head north along Broad Walk, to the right of the palace to the Sunken Garden (19), **also known as a Dutch Garden.**

19

The garden was designed in 1908 with walkways around the garden, curved branched trees and benches to relax on – in the evening, fairy lights switch on.

Back on Broad Walk, walk north to the park exit.

You will pass The Orangery shortly on the left built in 1704-5 – the building held parties and was also a conservatory for delicate plants in the winter. Today it is an excellent restaurant.

Further along is a carousel and a café, and the entrance to the Diana Memorial Playground (20). The Playground opened in 2000 and today receives over 1 million visitors each year. It has a light Peter Pan theme with a pirate ship and a beach. The playground remembers Diana, Princess of Wales, and her love and work with children.

Just outside the entrance, accessible to all, is the Elfin Oak. It was designed by Ivor Innes in 1930 and is made from the trunk of a 900-year-old oak tree brought from Richmond Park in south London. The sculpture has small figures carved into it including elves and gnomes.

Continue north up Broad Walk to exit Kensington Gardens. Cross the road and turn right. Queensway station is on the next corner. This is where our tour ends.

Walk 7: Knightsbridge and South Kensington Walk

Walk Length: 4.5 km / 2.8 mi
Timings: 1h 45m (fast), 2h (regular), 2h 15m (leisurely)
Start: Knightsbridge station
End: High Street Kensington station

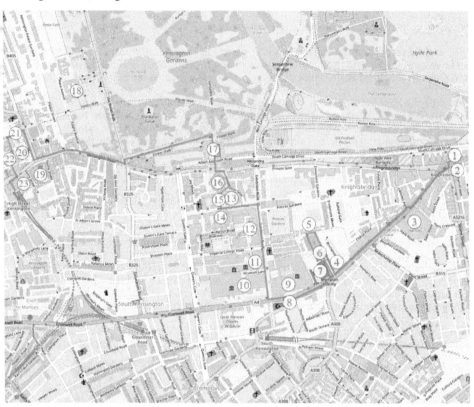

(1) Mandarin Oriental Hotel
(2) Harvey Nichols
(3) Harrods
(4) Brompton Road Tube Station
(5) Ennismore Garden Mews
(6) Holy Trinity Brompton
(7) Brompton Oratory
(8) Yalta Memorial Garden
(9) Victoria and Albert Museum
(10) Natural History Museum
(11) Science Museum
(12) Imperial College London

(13) Albert Court
(14) Royal College of Music
(15) Memorial for Exhibition of 1851
(16) Royal Albert Hall
(17) Albert Memorial
(18) Kensington Palace
(19) Barkers
(20) St. Mary Abbots church
(21) Holland Street
(22) St Mary Abbots Church Gardens
(23) The Roof Gardens

Begin at Knightsbridge station – there are several exits. You will need Exit 1 for the Mandarin Oriental Hotel.

You are now standing next to one of the busiest roads in West London, Knightsbridge.

The building to your left is the 5-star Mandarin Oriental Hotel (1). The building originally opened in 1889 as a gentlemen's club and re-opened in 1902 as the Hyde Park Hotel, before it was bought in 1996 and re-opened in its current guise in 2000 as the Mandarin Oriental.

The original entrance to the hotel was on the park side, though today it is on Knightsbridge – the old entrance round the back as designated as a royal entrance and permission must be sought from the Royal Parks to use it; this is occasionally granted today for special occasions.

Opposite the Mandarin Oriental, stands one of London's finest department stores – Harvey Nichols (2). The store started in 1831 by Benjamin Harvey on its current site, though with a much smaller footprint – originally only linen was sold. Over the years, the store expanded into the neighbouring properties and was subsequently rebuilt from scratch as one store in 1889, and now sells all manner of luxury goods.

Knightsbridge runs to the left between Harvey Nichols and the Mandarin Oriental. The name does not, in fact, have anything to with knights – the area in Old English was known as "Cnihtebricge" for example in 1050 and as "Knyghtesbrugg" by 1364 likely meaning a bridge where young men or horsemen congregated.

Knightsbridge is today one of London's wealthiest areas with extremely expensive real estate and a huge selection of luxury shopping. Nowhere is this better seen than with the modern glass building to the right of the station. This is One Hyde Park, where the least expensive properties start at £20 million, and £50 million is common for a 5-bed flat. There are newspaper reports of a property selling here for £140 million covering 20,000 square feet, making it the most expensive residential property ever sold in the world at the time.

Ahead, the street running past the side of Harvey Nichols is Sloane Street, which is filled with luxury shopping and ends in the fashionable district of Sloane Square 1km south of here.

Head down Brompton Road to the right where you will soon reach Knightsbridge's most famous luxury shop – Harrods (3).

Harrods was established by Charles Henry Harrod in 1824 in Southwark, South London – not far from where The Shard stands today. The shop specialised in drapery. By 1832, Harrods was dabbling in the grocery business with a shop in Clerkenwell, followed by a wholesale grocer just 2 years later in Whitechapel.

It was not until 1849 that Harrod opened his first shop on its current site on Brompton Road, designed to capitalise on the nearby Great Exhibition of 1851 (a topic we will return to later in this tour) which was expended to draw huge crowds.

By 1880, the shop had expanded rapidly from one room to multiple buildings joined together and a staff of over 100 people.

The shop changed hands many times over the years and was famously owned by Mohammed Al Fayed and his brother from 1985 to 2010. Mohammed Al Fayed's son Dodi Fayed dated Diana Spencer after her divorce with Prince Charles.

Harrods housed England's first escalator (or "moving staircase"); most visitors were so scared of using the contraption that Harrods began offering brandy to calm the nerves of those who rode it.

Today, Harrods is the biggest department store in Europe, with 330 departments and retail space of 1 million ft2 (90,000 m2). It is worth exploring to see the incredible variety of extravagant things on offer, and the beautiful food court has to be seen to be believed.

Harrods held four Royal Warrants, confirming they supplied the Royal Family. These were awarded by Queen Elizabeth II, the Queen Mother, Prince Charles and Prince Philip. However, in 2000 (three years after Diana and Dodi's death), Prince Philip removed his warrant. Harrods and the Royal family severed all ties as Al Fayed believed the Royal Family were responsible for his son's and Diana's deaths. The 2011 film "Unlawful Killing: The Murder of Princess Diana" shows footage of Al Fayed burning his Royal Warrants in a bonfire close to his son's grave. Today, there are currently two memorials remembering Diana Spencer and Dodi Fayed in the basement of the shop (follow signs to the Egyptian Escalator), though these are expected to be removed in 2018.

Continue down Brompton Road past Harrods. Cross to the other side of the street and walk for approximately 400m until you reach Cottage Place. Immediately on your right are the red ox-blood tiles of an abandoned London Underground station.

This was the site of Brompton Road Tube Station (4), which opened in 1906 and closed just 28 years later in 1934, During WWII, it was used by the then-owner the Ministry of Defence as a command centre. Its closure was largely due to its lack of use with Knightsbridge and South Kensington Stations being a short walk away. The station was designed by Leslie Green. The site was sold for £53 million in 2014 and the intention is to redevelop the land into residential use.

4

Continue along Cottage Place, past a row of garages. The road soon ends but you can continue on the footpath passing by a church and a garden (we will return to these shortly) until you reach the colourful houses of Ennismore Garden Mews (5).

So far on this walk, we have seen the busier parts of Knightsbridge and Kensington along the main Brompton Road. This residential area, however, gives you an insight into why people choose to live here. These streets are an oasis of calm is what is such a busy area – harkening back to the days of when this was a mere village a few miles from London. The arrival of the Underground in the area in 1868 changed all that, though substantial redevelopment had been happening nearby in Belgravia since the early 19th century.

5

Properties are by no means cheap here, particularly considering these streets (mews) were once used to house the servants and horses of wealthy residents. In 2014, number 2 Ennismore Garden Mews sold for just shy of £4 million pounds. It is undoubtedly worth at least £5 million in early 2018 at the time of writing – compared to the apartments at One Hyde Park, however, these properties seem like a bargain.

Make your way into the gardens and follow the map to Holy Trinity Brompton (6).

This small Anglican church was consecrated in 1829, and was designed by Thomas Leverton Donaldson. The style of worship here was described in The Guardian as "a noisy mini-reformation… with its rock-band style of worship, social activism and unabashed evangelical drive to make converts."

The current Archbishop of Canterbury who is the spiritual head of the Church of England, Justin Welby, began

6

his spiritual journey as part of the congregation at Holy Trinity Brompton.

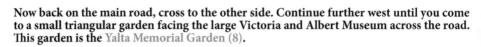

Continue walking through the park and alongside the much larger Brompton Oratory (7) **towards the main road. Take a peek inside if you**

Brompton Oratory is one of the rare Catholic Churches in the centre of the city as many were changed to
Church of England. This church is the second largest
Catholic church in the capital (the largest is Westminster Cathedral); the width of the nave exceeding of this
church is larger than that of the magnificent St. Paul's
Cathedral (Church of England).

The church was consecrated in 1884 and was designed
by Herbert Gribble in a neo-classical Italian Baroque
style. Perhaps the most notable event of the 20th century was the wedding of director Alfred
Hitchcock and Alma Reville.

**Now back on the main road, cross to the other side. Continue further west until you come
to a small triangular garden facing the large Victoria and Albert Museum across the road.
This garden is the** Yalta Memorial Garden (8).

The garden, and also the sculpture called "Twelve Responses to Tragedy", remembers the
Yalta Conference held in February 1945 at the conclusion of WWII in which USA President
Franklin D. Roosevelt, British Prime Minister Winston Churchill and Soviet Union Premier
Joseph Stalin met to discuss the future of Germany and Europe's post-war reorganisation. This
memorial commemorates the people who were displaced as a result of this conference. The
current sculpture dates from 1986.

Immediately across the road is the beautiful Victoria and Albert Museum (9), the largest art
and design museum in the world spanning 12.5 acres. The museum will easily take you several
days to explore in its entirety, and has over 4.5 million objects on display spanning over 5000
years – admission is free.

The Victoria and Albert Museum (V&A) was es-
tablished in 1852 and was originally known as the
Museum of Manufactures at Marlborough House near
Buckingham Palace. The collection later moved to
Somerset House and in 1857 it opened as the South
Kensington Museum on its current site.

The museum promoted itself as a place for education
and in 1858 introduced late night openings which were
described as "most convenient [hours to visit for] the
working classes". In 1899, when laying the foundation stone for an expansion of the museum
and in the presence of Queen Victoria it was announced that the museum would be renamed
the Victoria and Albert Museum.

You are now in the museum district, as you will shortly see. This area is also known as Albertopolis after Prince Albert. To understand why the museums came to this area, we must look
to 1851 and The Great Exhibition which took place in Hyde Park inside an enormous glass
structure known as the Crystal Palace. It was the first World's Fair and was the brainchild of Sir
Henry Cole (a civil servant and inventor) and Prince Albert, Queen Victoria's husband.

The exhibition was primarily concerned with showcasing the latest in technological and industrial innovation to the public as well as exhibiting Britain's dominance in this respect. The
exhibition was incredibly popular, amassing over 6 million visitors – a third of the country's
population at the time, and made a profit of £186,000 – equivalent to about £18.5 million in
2018's money.

Using this money, the area to the south of Hyde Park was purchased by the Royal Commission

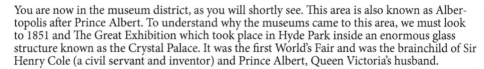

or the Exhibition of 1851 with the intention of turning it into an educational and cultural venue for all. The term "Albertopolis" is rarely used by anyone other than historians, and most people simply refer to the area by its tube station's name, "South Kensington".

Continue alongside the main road and cross over so you are on the side of the road with the V&A. Then follow Exhibition Road named after the Great Exhibition of 1851. Cross onto the left side of this road for a view of the Natural History Museum (10).

The Natural History Museum is the area's youngest major museum, dating from 1881. The museum owes much of its creation to palaeontologist Richard Owen, who was superintendent of the natural history departments of the British Museum. Owen felt his departments had outgrown their space in the British Museum and soon it was decided a dedicated building would be needed.

The building the NHM is housed in was designed by Alfred Waterhouse in a Romanesque style with terracotta tiles both inside and out. The building's architecture had led to the museum sometimes described as a "cathedral of nature". Several extensions have been added over the years including the eight-storey cocoon-shaped Darwin Centre first opened in 2002.

Today the museum houses 80 million items covering five main themes: plants, insects, minerals, fossils and animals. Admission is free, though waits can be lengthy – particularly during school holidays as it is the most popular of the three major museums in the area.

Continue along Exhibition Road northwards with a great view of the side of the Victoria and Albert Museum. Shortly ahead, on the same side of the road as the NHM lies the Science Museum (11).

London's Science Museum is the last of our three major museums in Albertopolis/South Kensington. The museum was founded in 1857 by Bennet Woodcroft from the collection of the Royal Society of Arts, and items from the 1851 Great Exhibition. The Science Museum eventually became its own independent entity in 1909. The current building was finished in 1928.

Today's collection spans over 300,000 items including the first jet engine, Stephenson's Rocket – an early steam locomotive and even the first prototype of the Clock of the Long Now – a clock designed to keep time for 10,000 years. Admission to the museum is free.

Almost immediately opposite you will see the tall golden-coloured spire of the Hyde Park Chapel Church of Jesus Christ of Latter Day Saints (a Mormon church). Continue slightly further ahead and soon on the left you will come to a modern building – Imperial College London (12).

Imperial College owes its foundation to Prince Albert, having been created with some of the funds of The Great Exhibition. Then called the Imperial Institute, it was created in 1887 o celebrate Queen Victoria's Jubilee and to promote industrial research throughout the British Empire. In 1907, the Board of Education found that there was a greater capacity for higher technical education and through the merger of several institutions, The Imperial College of Science and Technology was formed that same year.

Today Imperial College London is regarded as one of the country's best academic institutions. Notable alumni include Sir Alexander Fleming who discovered penicillin, Peter Higgs known for the Higgs Boson particle and author H. G. Wells.

At the roundabout with the Jamaican High Commission on the corner, turn left head down Prince Consort Road.

Opposite the white stone building of Imperial College is the beautiful high-rise red-brick Albert Court (13), one of the many Gothic Revival Victorian mansion blocks in the area.

Victorian mansion blocks, like this one, were built in the mid-to-late nineteenth century as land in the areas fashionable with the rich was scarce. The idea of flats or apartments was, however, deeply unpopular, however, as these were seen as accommodation for the poorer classes and foreigners.

Mansion blocks were therefore created as large luxury homes unlike many apartments today – most have several bedrooms, high ceilings, large interiors and often marble hallways.

There are also almost always extra amenities for residents such as porters, a concierge service and possibly even a private rooftop garden. Very often these are not just called flats but "mansion flats" alluding to their expansive interiors. As a guide price, a 3-bed (3,000 ft2 or 270 m2) flat will sell anywhere from £8 million to £12.5 million in Albert Court. A 5-bed in this block recently sold for £21 million.

The tragedy of Albertopolis was the Prince Albert never saw it completed, as he died in December 1861 just ten years after starting this major project. Albert died at Windsor Castle at the age of just 42 – the contemporary diagnosis was for Typhoid Fever, though today it is thought his illness had in fact been ongoing for at least two years by the time of his death, indicating another cause of death such as Crohn's disease, kidney failure or abdominal cancer.

Victoria and Albert were deeply in love and Albert's death, combined with her mother's death earlier that year led to Victoria going into a deep state of mourning. She placed herself in isolation, avoided public appearances (including 4 years of State Opening of Parliament ceremonies) and wore black for the rest of her life. She lived for a further 40 years without her husband and a large part of today's Albertopolis was built under the command of Queen Victoria as a way of honouring her husband.

Continue past Albert Court and cross to the other side, climb the steps to the right with a magnificent view of the enormous Royal Albert Hall. Half way up the steps it is worth looking back away from the Royal Albert Hall to the Royal College of Music (14).

The Royal College of Music was founded in 1883 replacing the National Training School for Music dating from just a few years earlier in 1876, this was from a much earlier proposal by Prince Albert to provide free musical training to winners of scholarships. The current building dates from the 1890s and was designed by Sir Arthur Blomfield in the Flemish Mannerist style. Today the college teaches Western music from an undergraduate to doctoral level, and also has a Saturday school for children.

Continue up the steps to the Royal Albert Hall where you will see the Memorial for the Exhibition of 1851 (15).

Originally this memorial was designed to be dedicated to The Great Exhibition and a statue of Britannia (Britain in woman form) was meant to crown the memorial. However, after Albert's death, Queen Victoria requested that Joseph Durham's memorial be changed to include a statue of Albert on top instead.

The memorial was first installed here in 1863 when this site was a horticultural garden, though it has been re-sited several times due to development of the area surrounding it. The memorial is made of Aberdeen and Cornish granite with bronze female figures representing Europe, America, Asia and Africa.

Behind the memorial stands the magnificent Royal Albert Hall (16), a concert venue completed in 1871 – ten years after Albert's death as a visionary memorial to the man who helped make Albertopolis a reality. The hall was designed to accommodate 8,000 people; however, modern safety standards restrict this to just over 5,500. Around the outside of the building is a mosaic frieze, depicting "The Triumph of Arts and Sciences".

Today "The Nation's Village Hall", as it is sometimes called, holds a variety of events such as classical music concerts as part of the BBC Proms series each summer, circus performances by Cirque du Soleil and even film premieres such as that of Star Wars: The Last Jedi in December 2017.

Head around the Royal Albert Hall to the right hand side until you are at the front by the busy Kensington Road. Use the pedestrian crossing here to enter Kensington Gardens and head up the steps to the Albert Memorial (17) **in the park. You can get some great photos of the Royal Albert Hall looking back here too.**

The Albert Memorial, unsurprisingly, remembers Prince Albert and commemorates his life and achievements. It was unveiled in 1872 and the gilt bronze statue in the centre of Albert seated was added in 1875. The memorial took an incredible 10 years to build – compare that to the mere 4 years it took to build the Royal Albert Hall.

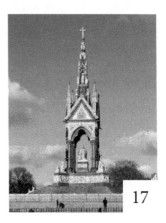

The memorial's designer was famed architect Sir George Gilbert Scott and it was created in the Gothic Revival style. The statue of Albert looks south towards Albertopolis.

Under the statue of Albert is the Frieze of Parnassus, which depicts 169 composers, architects, poets, painters, and sculptors. Each statue is life-size. The frieze was sculpted by Henry Hugh Armstead and John Birnie Philip. Carvings were made on the memorial itself "in situ". The south side, facing the Royal Albert Hall, is deemed the most important

17

as it is "the front" and shows poets and musicians, as in Victorian England poetry was deemed the finest of arts.

The triangular mosaic section by the "roof" depicts pictures of allegorical figures representing the four aforementioned forms of art (poetry, painting, architecture and sculpture). Near the top of the canopy's tower are eight statues of virtues: Faith, Hope, Charity and Humility, Fortitude, Prudence, Justice and Temperance.

On the four corners above the frieze are four sets of statues celebrating industry – agriculture, commerce, engineering and manufacturing. On the outer four corners, there are four more sets of statues for four continents: Europe, Africa, Asia and the Americas. With all this, the memorial is as much about Albert as it is about the dominance of the British empire.

Continue round the Albert Memorial to the other side. Head down the pathway at the back and turn left through a gate into the Flower Walk – a pleasant route through this south side of the park as opposed to busy Kensington Road. Once you get reach the end of Flower Walk you will be on Broad Walk. Notice Kensington Palace (18) **to the right, the red-brick building. The Palace is spoken about in detail in Walk 6.**

Turn left to exit the park and continue to the right along Kensington Road, going westwards with the park on your right hand side. Continue past the park until you see a large white building on the left with a tower saying 'Barkers' (19) **at the top.**

Barkers was a department store started by John Barker and James Whitehead in 1870. It was initially started as a small drapery business but by 1900 the business had expanded to a whole city block. The current building (designed by Bernard George) was constructed in phases between 1930 and 1957, construction having been halted by the Blitz. The store's popularity started to wane and it continually downsized from the 1970s until its eventual closure in 2006 after over 135 years in business. Today the ground floor is a Whole Food Market and much of the building is home to DMG Media which publishes the Daily Mail and Metro, among other newspapers.

Take the next right down Kensington Church Street.

The magnificent St. Mary Abbots church (20) is here on the corner. Designed by Sir George Gilbert Scott, who also designed the Albert Memorial from earlier, the present church was built in 1872 and has the tallest spire in London at 278 feet (85 m). It is a mix of early English and neo-Gothic styles.

20

The first church was built on this site in 1262. The Norman church was then rebuilt in 1370 and replaced again in the late 17th century; the surrounding area had become fashionable, as William III had moved to living in nearby Kensington Palace. Today's church still contains many monuments from the mid-1600s and five of the bells which are rung date from 1772.

Follow Kensington Church Street north. Take the first left onto Holland Street (21).

This is the fringe of a district called Holland Park within the borough of Kensington and Chelsea. Most of this area was once part of the grounds of a mansion called Holland House (or Cope Castle) built in 1605 – the house was home to various Earls of Holland over the years.

The area is today home to some of the most expensive property in the world, and is home to many British celebrities including Richard Branson and David and Victoria Beckham. At the time of writing there is a 10-bedroom house on the market for £30 million and a 6-bedroom house for £21.5 million in the area.

There is also an actual park called Holland Park which is well worth a visit after this tour and is located just a 5-minute walk west along Kensington High Street from the end point of this tour.

On Holland Street, turn left down Kensington Church Walk – this is on the corner of the brick buildings and the first white house. Continue past the shops and the mural into the St Mary Abbots Church Gardens (22) for an amazing view of one of the church entrances. Continue along the path passing a small park before emerging onto Kensington High Street.

Immediately opposite, across the road, the large white building ahead home to Marks and Spencer was, until recently, the location of the Kensington Roof Gardens (23).

The site was free to access and included 3 different gardens: a Spanish Garden, a Tudor-style garden and an English woodland garden home to pintail ducks and flamingos. Admission was via event invitations, eating at the restaurant, or in the day you could simply walk in when events were not on.

After 37 years of operating, Virgin Group closed The Roof Gardens (23) in January 2018. It is not known if it will reopen to the public, but it is worth checking online as it is such a unique experience.

22

To the right of Marks and Spencer is High Street Kensington Station where this tour concludes.

If you wish to visit Holland Park now (with the Kyoto Japanese Garden with peacocks, and the free Design Museum), turn right. There is a park entrance about 5 minutes' walk away (500 m) on the right.

Walk 8: The City of London and Bankside

Walk Length: 4.0 km / 2.5 mi
Timings: 2h (fast), 2h 30m (regular), 3h (leisurely)
Start: St. Paul's station
End: Aldgate station

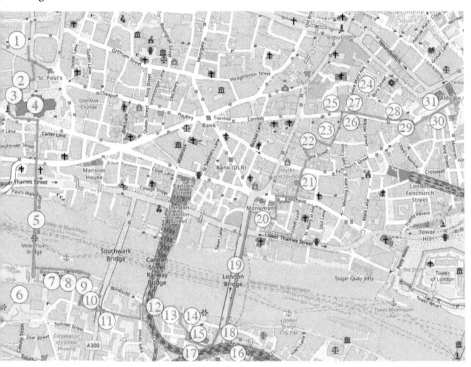

1) Christchurch Greyfriars	(17) Borough Market
2) Paternoster Square	(18) The Spike
3) Temple Bar	(19) London Bridge
4) St. Paul's Cathedral	(20) The Monument
5) Millennium Bridge	(21) The Walkie Talkie
6) Tate Modern	(22) Leadenhall Market
7) Row of Houses	(23) Lloyd's of London
8) Shakespeare's Globe Theatre	(24) The Gherkin
9) Bear Gardens	(25) The Cheesegrater
10) The Rose Theatre	(26) The Scalpel
11) Original site of The Globe	(27) St. Andrew Undershaft
12) The Clink Prison	(28) St. Katherine Kree
13) Ruins of Winchester Palace	(29) Aldgate Pump
14) Golden Hinde II	(30) Site of Aldgate
15) Southwark Cathedral	(31) St. Botolph without Aldgate
16) The Shard	

This tour begins at St. Paul's station, use Exit Number 2.

You are now in an area of London called the "City of London". This area, just over 1 mile2 in size, is the financial heart of London and, at the time of writing, the largest financial centre in the world. Amongst all the shiny skyscrapers, there is an area steeped in history as this area is where the Romans first settled around AD 43-47 – at the time, the area became known as "Londinium".

In this walk when referring to London as a whole, we call it a "city" (small 'c'), whereas when referring to this particular part of London, it is the "City" (capital 'c'). This area is also often called "the square mile". The City's local authority which manages the area is called The City of London Corporation, which is thought to be the world's oldest continuously-elected local government authority.

Turn left outside St. Paul's station – we will start of this walk with an often overlooked gem. At the junction with the first pedestrian crossing (note the London Stock Exchange building here), cross to the traffic island and again to an unusual looking church.

This is Christchurch Greyfriars (1). The original church was established here in the thirteenth century, and was rebuilt after the Great Fire of 1666 (more on this later in the walk) with the design by architect Christopher Wren – this is a name you will get used to reading about as Wren was responsible for over 50 church rebuilds in the area, as well as several other major projects throughout London.

This incarnation of the church was completed in 1687, with a steeple added in 1704 standing 160 feet (49m) tall. Several modifications were also made to the design in the eighteenth century.

Unfortunately, despite standing for over 250 years, on 29 December 1940 during The Blitz of WWII a firebomb hit the church and burnt much of the church to the ground. It is a testament to The City of London Corporation that it still stands today. Especially, in an area desperate for land to build new skyscrapers. The Corporation has an incredible amount of respect for tradition and maintaining its historical sites as shall be seen throughout this walk.

Today Christ Church Greyfriars is a very well-maintained public garden with the old church tower and the walls which survived The Blitz framing the space.

Retrace your steps back to near the London Stock Exchange and walk down Queen's Head Passage on the right towards St. Paul's Cathedral. Before reaching the cathedral (which we will see later), take the first right onto Paternoster Square (2). In the centre stands the Paternoster Square column.

The square is a relatively space for London developed between 1995 and 2003, and gets its name from a street called Paternoster Row which stood here and was destroyed during The Blitz. The old street is named after the monks who during their processions would recite the Lord's Prayer, in which the first line in Latin is "Pater Noster". In the nineteenth century the area was famous for its roaring book trade.

The centre of the square is dominated by the 75 ft (23m) tall Paternoster Square Column, which remembers both the Great Fire of London and the fire during the Blitz which destroyed this square – it bares a striking resemblance to a monument we shall see later in the tour. The monument was designed at the same time as the square and if you look closely by the steps you will see grates, as this monument cleverly doubles up as a ventilation shaft for the road and car park underneath.

70

As you came into the square you may also have noticed a statue of a person herding sheep. This sculpture, designed by Elizabeth Frink, dates from 1975 and was moved here in 2003. It remembers when this area was home to Newgate Meat Market between the late 17th century and the mid-18th century. It was replaced by Smithfield Market nearby in 1868.

Exit the square to the south side towards St. Paul's Cathedral via an archway. This is Temple Bar (3).

Temple Bar once stood at the other end of Fleet Street, near the Royal Courts of Justice, approximately 800 m west of this point. It was designed by Christopher Wren (rebuilt in 1672 after the Great Fire) and marked the western-most point of The City of London's boundaries. The Temple Bar Gate House's job was to restrict and control entry into the City of London. It stood until 1878 when it was moved to a park and was left to decay. In 2004, it was re-erected in its current location at a cost of £3 million.

Once through the archway you will find yourself with a magnificent view of St. Paul's Cathedral (4) **and, in particular, the Cathedral's famous dome. A door ahead leads to the crypt café and toilets if you need a rest stop. Feel free to either stand here to read the next section or turn right and head to the front of the church with its famed steps.**

St. Paul's Cathedral is strategically placed here at the top of Ludgate Hill, the highest point of the City of London. The origins of the first church on this site dedicated to Paul the Apostle date back to AD 604. The hilltop location served two purposes, it allowed churchgoers to be "closer to God" and, more practically, also made sure the church wouldn't flood at high tide.

Today's St Paul's Cathedral building was designed, unsurprisingly, by Sir Christopher Wren – it is his grandest church, a true architectural masterpiece rebuilt after The Great Fire of London and finished in 1710.

Measuring 365-feet tall, St. Paul's Cathedral can be seen from much of the surrounding area and from across London where designated sightlines prevent anything from obstructing the view of the Cathedral, hence the unusual shape of many of London's skyscrapers. The City believes that despite being in a financial district dominated by enormous skyscrapers, St. Paul's should never be obscured. It was the tallest building in London from 1710 until 1967.

At the top is the Golden Gallery (528 steps up) where visitors can get an incredible view of central London – you can look west towards Westminster and the London Eye, to the north is the Barbican Centre, east reveals The City's impressive skyscrapers, as well as Tower Bridge, whilst to the south lies The Shard, Shakespeare's Globe Theatre and The Tate Modern. As well as the viewing area at the Golden Gallery, the Stone Gallery further down provides a good view. Other areas of note include The Crypt, the interior dome, and the Geometric Staircase.

The church has also staged many major ceremonies – the marriage of Diana Spencer and Prince Charles, thanksgiving services for the Queen's jubilees, as well as the funerals of Winston Churchill, Margaret Thatcher and Admiral Nelson.

In fiction, the steps of St. Paul's were also famously recreated on a film set in California and used in Mary Poppins' "Feed the Birds" sequence.

There is a charge to enter the church, currently £18 on the door, which includes a multimedia guided tour. On Sundays, you can enter and briefly see the Cathedral inside without paying. Only a small part of the nave is accessible and there is no touring on this day. Services are free to access on all days. If touring, you should allow about 2 hours to see the church in its entirety, including climbing to the top. St. Paul's Cathedral is the largest church in London, and the second largest church building in the UK after Liverpool Cathedral.

Head round the cathedral to the right, past the steps at the front and The City information centre on your right. Follow the map until you are on the other side of the road. You will pass the College of Arms on your right, built in the 1670s. Cross over and head towards the Millennium Bridge. Head down Peter's Hill, crossing over Queen Victoria Street and continue down Sermon Lane until you are on the Millennium Bridge (5).

The Millennium Bridge had a fraught beginning and is now nicknamed the "Wobbly Bridge" due to an engineering oversight when it was first unveiled. On its opening day, as people crossed the bridge, their walking patterns caused the bridge to sway from side to side.

5

As the bridge swayed and people matched their foot-steps to maintain their balance, the swaying intensified in an effect known as "synchronous lateral excitation". The bridge had to be closed only 2 days after opening to fix this issue, and re-opened only two years later with the problem fixed.

Potter fans may recognise the bridge from the sixth Harry Potter film where it is destroyed by Death Eaters.

Cross the bridge onto the south side of the river, walking towards the building with the tall tower. This is the Tate Modern Art Gallery (6).

6

Originally, the Bankside Power Station, it generated electricity from 1891 to 1981. By the 1970s, rising oil prices made the power station uneconomical compared to its coal-powered competitors and it closed in 1981. The building remained unused until The Tate Gallery began work on the building in 1995 for its Tate Modern Art Gallery. An extension to the art gallery opened in 2016.

Admission is free, except to temporary exhibitions. Inside you will find international modern and contemporary art dating from 1900 until today. The restaurant at the top of the original building has magnificent views over towards The City, or you can get an equally good view at no cost from the viewing gallery at the top of the New Tate Modern ("The Switch House").

At the end of the Millennium Bridge, you descend down a ramp to reach Bankside with magnificent views towards St. Paul's Cathedral. Turn right when exiting the bridge ramp (going East) and you will see a small row of houses (7) on the right hand side.

Number 49 (the tall white house) Cardinal's Wharf has a plaque outside saying that this was where Christopher Wren lived during the construction of St. Paul's Cathedral, and also where Catherine of Aragon took shelter on her arrival in London.

7

However, Gillian Tindall, a writer and historian discovered that this plaque was only added in the mid-twentieth century and then Wren had in fact lived a few doors further east. One man who did, however, actually live in the house – more recently – was Robert Stevenson, director of Disney's "Mary Poppins".

Number 49 was, in fact, built in 1710 – the same year as the completion of St. Paul's, making the Catherine of Aragon story also untrue. Tindall's theory is that Malcolm Munth, the building's owner in 1945, retrieved the plaque when the original Wren building was demolished and placed it on No.49 to protect it from demolition. It is, perhaps, due to this new "fake history" that the house still stands today.

The red-brick building to its right, number 51, dates back to 1712. The late Dean of Southwark, Reverend Colin Slee, lived at the property until his death in 2010, while No.52 was a residence for the Cathedral's director of music. In case you're wondering how much one of these houses would set you back: No. 51 was listed for sale at £6 million in 2011.

Continue further ahead and soon, on your right, is Shakespeare's Globe Theatre (8).

Shakespeare's Globe is undoubtedly one of the most famous theatres in London, if not the world. Home to performances by The Bard, you may be surprised to hear that the theatre in front of you in not the original, nor the second, and is in fact a replica from 1997 – and it's not even on the same site!

The original theatre, the wooden Globe Theatre, was built in 1599 by Shakespeare's play company the Lord Chamberlain's Men. However, during a performance of *Henry VIII* in 1613, a canon was fired and the theatre burnt to the ground – remarkably everyone inside the theatre escaped alive. A second Globe Theatre was built in 1614 but was closed by Puritans in 1642 who thought theatres were sinful. It was demolished shortly thereafter.

Today's "Shakespeare's Globe" was the pet project of Sam Wanamaker, an American actor who was surprised to hear that The Globe no longer existed and there had been no attempt to honour Shakespeare in London. His objective was to built a faithful reconstruction of the original, but there are very few records as to what the first Globe Theatre looked like. Instead, the theatre we see today is based on the design of London's first theatre – creatively called "The Theatre" – with other details incorporated from further research. The project was completed in 1997, 4 years after Wanamaker's death, and the structure is made of wood like the original and was built using techniques employed during the construction of the original theatre.

The location of today's theatre is in fact much better than the original; being on the embankment by the River Thames, it is visible to passing boats and even has a pier right outside. The site of the original Globe Theatre is just a short walk away from this location, and we shall see it later in the tour. It would not have been possible to build the original Globe in this location as the River Thames at the time was wider than it is today.

The Shakespeare Globe is a fantastic place to feel what it was like to watch a Shakespeare play at the time. The seating is in the same style, with a standing 'pit' area where tickets cost just £5. Seats are often sold out months in advance. The theatre has no roof to allow sunlight in, speech is done without microphones and electrical instruments and amplification are avoided. Due to the exposure to the elements, Shakespeare's Globe only operates in the summer. A, indoor theatre, The Sam Wanamaker playhouse, was added in 2014 and provides candlelit performances even during the colder months.

The tour of the Shakespeare Globe theatre and the exhibition on Shakespeare himself is also an excellent visit, and both are open year-round. There is an admission charge for these.

Continue east along Bankside two roads further until you reach a small gap between two buildings called Bear Gardens (9).

Since you stepped off the Millennium Bridge, you also left the City of London and are now in the London Borough of Southwark.

Southwark, being outside the original stone City walls, was never subject to its laws and from the 14th century onwards was well known as an entertainment district. It was not the safest area of London, however, with theatres, brothels and prisons. Whereas some of these forms of entertainment have remained, others have been lost in time. One of those is Bear-baiting, which was a common event in London and give this street its name.

Bear-baiting was usually performed in theatres called beargardens or bear pits, similar to playhouses, and events would attract large crowds – its heyday was in the 16th and 17th centuries. The show involved animal cruelty including whipping bears, bulls throwing dogs into the air, horses with apes tied to their backs, all for the amusement of spectators.

Upon entering Bear Gardens, take a look to the wall on the left for the Ferrymans Seat.

This mysterious artefact unfortunately cannot be dated back to a particular period, but we do know what it was used for. On this spot, before there were so may bridges across the Thames, ferrymen used to provide ferry boat services across the river. This seat was one of many where these men waited when plying for trade.

Head up Bear Gardens. Today this is a rather unremarkable alleyway with the backs of shops, though it once was the epicentre of the beat baiting trade at the Davies Amphitheatre, the last bear baiting pit in London. At the end of the street, turn left onto Park Street. Shortly on the left just before the overhead bridge look out for a Blue Plaque marking the site of The Rose Theatre (10)**.**

The Rose was the first public playhouse in Southwark and the fourth ever built in London. The theatre was built in 1587 by Philip Henslowe and John Cholmley. It was the first purpose-built playhouse to ever stage a production of any of Shakespeare's plays. The theatre had 14 sides and measured about 72 feet (22 m) in diameter. The theatre was destroyed in the early 17th century when the lease for the land came up for renewal and the landowners wanted three times the price paid for the previous lease.

In 1989, the ruins of The Rose were threatened with destruction by property development – a building now stands on this site but archaeologists were able to excavate during its construction. In 1999 the site reopened to the public and you can see the original theatre foundations inside – a new indoor venue was created which performs plays, commonly by Shakespeare.

Continue east along Park Street. Just after the overhead bridge on the right hand side is an area remembering the original site of The Globe Theatre (11) **with several plaques remembering this. Today the site is, sadly, a bland car park between two buildings – there is, however, a silver plaque on the ground in a partial circle, indicating where The Globe would have stood.**

11

Continue down Park Street, turn left onto Bank End and go ahead. Stop by the passageway under the railways bridge on your right hand side.

Just on the left side corner, before turning right under the bridge is The Anchor pub, the last surviving of the Bankside's inns which stood by the river. The pub claims to have been built in 1616, though it was destroyed in a fire in the 17th century and was rebuilt again in the 19th century. It is a fairly standard chain pub but does have a nice riverside terrace.

You may also have noticed on the railway arches a mural of William Shakespeare. It was designed by artist Jimmy C. and appeared in October 2016 as a celebration of 400 years of Shakespeare. Jimmy C. also painted another mural in Brixton to the late David Bowie which has proved incredibly popular with the singer's fans.

Continue under the railway arches until you reach the The Clink Prison (12) **museum.**

This museum is roughly on the site of the notorious Clink Prison, which stood here between 1151 and 1780 on land owned by the Bishop of Winchester – by the 1600s the prison was mainly used for those who had views contrary to those of the bishops, and towards the end of its operational use this was a debtors' prison whereby prisoners with a debt had to work to pay their way out or find funds from outside. To this day, we often use the expression "to send someone to The Clink" for sending someone to prison.

Continue along Clink Street which becomes Pickford Lane and you will soon see the ruins of Winchester Palace (13) **on your right.**

Winchester Palace was the home of the Bishop of Winchester – it was once one of the largest and most important buildings in the country and was first built in the 12th century, when most of both sides of the River Thames were spanned by large waterfront houses and mansions. The bishop of Winchester was the King's royal treasurer and so held a great amount of power.

Continue ahead past Winchester Palace until you reach the Golden Hinde II (14).

The remains you see today are of the Great Hall including the remains of a rose window - the palace was mostly destroyed by a fire in 1814, though by the 18th century the palace had been abandoned by royalty and was used as tenements and warehouses instead. The ruins have been viewable by the public since the area went through a large-scale redevelopment in the 1980s.

The Golden Hinde II is a full-size, historically accurate replica of Sir Francis Drake's galleon, the Golden Hinde, in which Drake became the first Englishman to circumnavigate around the world – a feat which took him 3 years between 1577 and 1580.

Queen Elizabeth I helped sponsor this voyage, and approved damage to the rival Spanish if needed. In 1579, in the Pacific Ocean, Golden Hinde challenged and captured the Spanish galleon Nuestra Señora de la Concepción, which had the largest treasure ever captured to that date: over 360,000 pesos (equivalent to around £480 million in 2017) including 26 tons of silver, and half a ton of gold.

To put the quantity of treasure into perspective over the voyage, around half of the treasure captured went to Elizabeth I - that 'half' is recorded as having been "enough to pay off [The queen's] entire government debt and still have £40,000 left over to invest in a new trading company". The ship was put on public display in a dockyard in Deptford, South London from 1580 until the 1650s, when it began to rot and it was eventually demolished. The best timber planks were converted into a chair in 1668, which still stands in the Bodlean Library at the University of Oxford to this day.

Today's replica Golden Hinde was built in 1973 and is the result of 3 years' research and construction. Since then, this replica has travelled more than 140,000 miles (225,000 km), including having circumnavigated around the world. The total mileage is the equivalent of going round the world more than five times, so, this replica may well have travelled further than the original.

The ship has been in its current location since 1996. Today this replica is an attraction open to visitors; during school holidays there are often actors on board, and there is occasionally even the option for an overnight sleepover on the galleon.

Head down Cathedral Street at the ship's front towards Southwark Cathedral (15) **ahead.**

It is difficult to ascertain when the first church was built on the site of today's Southwark Cathedral, but there are mentions of a minster here in the Domesday book (a survey) of 1086. We know that in 1106, the church became an Augustine priory under the patronage of the Bishops of Winchester.

However, the old church was damaged in a fire in 1212 and the layout of today's church was constructed between 1220 and 1420, making it the first Gothic church in London. The church was once again ravaged by fire in the 1390s and around 1420 it was partially rebuilt. Subsequent partial rebuilds and refurbishments in every century since have led to the church we see today. A large organ dates from 1897. The church was given cathedral status in 1905 when the Diocese of Southwark was created.

The church has links with several famous figures throughout history: William Shakespeare's brother, Edmund – an actor – was buried there in the church in 1607 and there is a stained-glass window and statue to William Shakespeare himself. John Harvard, who went on to found Harvard University in the USA, was baptised in the church in 1607 – there is a small chapel dedicated to him. There are also memorials inside to Nelson Mandela and Desmond Tutu.

Continue to the right around Southwark Cathedral, down Cathedral Street and soon to the left past the market and railway bridge is a skyscraper known as The Shard (16).

The Shard has become one of London's most iconic buildings since its completion in 2012. Standing at 310m (1016 ft) tall, with 95 floors, this is the tallest building in the UK. Upon its completion it was the tallest building in Europe, though at the time of writing it has now been surpassed by three buildings in Russia.

16

The built featured 72 habitable floors and was designed by Renzo Piano and has been nicknamed "a vertical city". The building features offices and retail towards the bottom third, 22 floors of hotel accommodation as part of the Shangri-La Hotel and restaurants, 13 floors of residence and an observatory from floor 68 to 72. The top 23 floors are the spire which are open to the elements in a design to resemble a shard of broken glass. Qatar owns 95% of the property; the rest is owned by UK-based Sellar Property Group.

The luxury flats in the building have not proven popular with buyers - in July 2017, five years after the building's opening, it was reported that none of the flats had been sold. Prices range from £30 million to £50 million. Initially Baron Phillips, spokesman for Irvine Sellar, had stated "I should think about 20 phone calls should do it, don't you?".

Back on ground level, you are now in the middle of Borough Market (17), which has been the site of a market since around 1014. Being near the pool of London (a former port nearby), the market was especially important during the Victorian era when London was a large port city.

The market is almost exclusively a food market with two distinct halves – the part on the right of this street (Cathedral Street) offers a full market like a supermarket might, as well as take-away food. The left hand part of the market is take-away only. On a warm day, this is a great place to stop for lunch and you will find it very busy at lunchtime daily, but particularly on Saturdays in the summer.

17

The market operates from Monday to Saturday from 10:00am to 5:00pm, with an early opening at 8:00am on Saturday, and late closing on Friday at 6:00pm. It is closed on Sundays.

Feel free to explore the market and once you have done so, walk through the market to the left until you find yourself along a busy road under the railway bridge, turn left and cross to the other side of the road – walk until you find yourself by the big spike (18).

18

This 16m-high spike, made of Portland stone, is tilted at 19.5 degrees and points at the spot where the old London Bridge used to stand. The next bridge built in 1831 was built to the side of it. The spike also serves as a reminder of the spikes which used to stand on London Bridge upon which heads of criminals were placed on top. It is even said that Scotsman William Wallace's head was placed on a spike on London Bridge.

In case you have not yet surmised, you are now standing on London Bridge (19).

Although many tourists, and indeed many Londoners, get their bridges confused, the more famous bridge in red, white and blue with two tall towers is called Tower Bridge and is a much more recent addition to London. We shall see it shortly.

The first few London Bridges were likely made of wood and appeared in the 1st century, when the Romans settled in London, with bridges being rebuilt throughout the centuries and replaced after destruction either by enemy or natural disaster. The first bridge historians know the most about is what we call "Old London Bridge" which stood from 1209 to 1831 and took 33 years to build.

The River Thames at the time was wider in many parts than it is today and the enormous bridge spanned 800-900 feet (240m to 270m) in length and was 26 feet (8m) wide. By the 1500s there were over 200 buildings located on the bridge itself and was effectively a street.

When the bridge was congested, crossing it could take up to an hour. Indeed, in 1722, congestion was so serious that the Lord Mayor requested that instead of traffic meandering left and right, all traffic drive to the left-hand side of their direction of travel – many believe this was the beginning of the practice of left-hand driving.

"New London Bridge" was the solution to the traffic problems and it was completed in 1831, 100 ft (30 m) west of the site of the old bridge. This bridge was 928 feet (283 m) long and 49 feet (15 m) wide and made from granite. By 1896, the bridge was used by 8000 pedestrians and 900 vehicles every hour and it was widened by a further 13 feet (4 m). However, the bridge had begun to sink and a replacement was needed.

In 1967, "New London Bridge" was put on the market for sale and was purchased by an oil entrepreneur called Robert P. McCulloch for $2.46 million. The bridge was taken apart, and each stone was numbered and shipped to the USA, where it was rebuilt in Lake Havasu City, Arizona. It still stands there to this day. Many believe that McCulloch purchased the bridge thinking he was buying the more majestic Tower Bridge instead, though this has been denied.

The London Bridge we have today was constructed from 1967 to 1972 and was officially opened in 1973 by Queen Elizabeth II. It is the same length as the bridge which it replaced and cost £4 million (£51.9 million in 2016) and is 104 feet (32 m) wide, almost double the width of the previous bridge adding much needed crossing capacity.

Finally, we could not talk about the bridge without mentioning the nursery rhyme "London Bridge is Falling Down" which is supposedly based on the many collapses of the bridges over the years, and specifically when London Bridge was destroyed by Olaf II of Norway in 1014.

While on the topic of songs, Fergie of Black Eyed Peas fame released a (not family-friendly) song called "London Bridge" in 2006, and incorrectly used a photo of Tower Bridge on her album cover instead of London Bridge.

Almost immediately after the spike on the south side of the bridge is a plinth on the pavement with a dragon on top – this is the City of London dragon which marks the boundary of the start of The City of London. You will find dragons at many entrances to The City by road and at the exit of some tube stations such as Bank. You are back in The City – look out for the dragons on bins, street signs, lampposts and even bus stops.

Cross London Bridge to the other side.

While on the bridge, you will see to the right HMS Belfast, a ship used in the D-Day Landings which is today a museum, as well as the more famous Tower Bridge dating from 1894, designed to relieve congestion on London Bridge. Walk Number 9 in this book contains much more detailed information on both of these monuments.

Across London Bridge, turn right onto Monument Street.

On Monument Street, you can see where the street's name comes from – the stone column ahead is called The Monument (20) or 'The Monument to the Great Fire of London'.

The Great Fire of London is a recurring theme in the history of London, as you may have noticed throughout this walk. The fire took place on Pudding Lane (seen shortly) in Thomas Farriner's bakery; Farriner was the King's baker.

Streets at the time in The City were extremely narrow, most buildings were made of wood, clean water was in very short supply and there was no formalised fire brigade service.

20

The fire began shortly after midnight on Sunday, 2nd September 1666. The main way of fighting fires at the time, due to the lack of water, was to create firebreaks in which houses were destroyed (usually with gunpowder) before the fire reach them; once the fire reached the destroyed houses, it had no fuel to keep going and it would die.

However, Sir Thomas Bloodworth (Lord Mayor of London) at the time, was so indecisive that it took him until the following evening to order that firebreaks be used. Initially, he claimed the fire was small remarking, "Pish! A woman could piss it out". By this point, it was too late and the fire continued to spread and burn, fuelled by the wind and continued until 6th September 1666. Officially, only between 6 and 8 people lost their lives as most fled. In total, 13,500 houses were destroyed, 87 parish churches, the old St. Paul's Cathedral and three City gatehouses.

A French watchmaker called Robert Hubert admitted to starting the fire, first claiming he had starting it in Westminster and then changing his story to Pudding Lane – he claimed The Pope had sent him. He was hanged for his crime, but it appears that Hubert had suffered from mental health difficulties. It also later emerged that he was on a ship at the time and had only arrived in London two days after the fire had started. Suspicion was rife that the fire had been started by a foreigner and Hubert's admission made him the perfect scapegoat.

Charles II requested a monument be built to remember the fire. The Monument is a 202-foot (61m) tall stone column and stands 202 feet away from where the fire started – it was unveiled in 1677 and is the tallest freestanding stone column in the world. Designed by Christopher Wren, today you can climb 311 steps up a spiral staircase for views from the top.

The current City of London was rebuilt largely on the old street layout with few modifications. Although new layouts by Wren and others had been proposed, they were deemed too complicated and expensive to build.

Many Londoners also believed the fire was an act of God and a warning against gluttony – the theory being that the fire had started on Pudding Lane and ended on Pye (Pie) Corner.

Walk past The Monument and take a left along Pudding Lane, where the Great Fire started. At the top turn right onto Eastcheap then left onto Philpot Lane. Soon on your right you will see a skyscraper known as The Walkie Talkie (21).

20 Fenchurch Street, often called The Walkie Talk due to its shape, stands at 34 stories and 160 m (525 ft) in height. This building is one of many in London which has had to be carefully

designed due to St. Paul's Cathedral being located nearby, approx. 1 km to the west. St. Paul's Cathedral is safeguarded by a policy known as "Protected Vistas" in which the Cathedral must be visible from certain spots in London, including King Henry's Mound an astonishing 15.5 km (9.6 mi) south-west of the cathedral. The views of the Cathedral may not be obscured, and buildings to the left and right of the cathedral (and behind it) are subject to restrictions. In the case of The Walkie Talkie, the original plans called for a 200m tall building, but this was reduced due to the visual intrusion it would cause – towering over St. Paul's from certain angle.

21

The construction process of the Walkie Talkie was also marked by an unfortunate incident. The building's unusual concave shape on its south side is covered entirely by glass and when the sun shines on it, it focuses the rays onto the street below. This resulted in at least two cars being damaged by the rays, including an owner of a Jaguar who, according to one newspaper, "found the wing mirror and panels had been damaged, parts of the car had 'buckled' and there was a smell of burning plastic." Shopkeepers reported blistered paint, a scorched plastic lemon and even a smoking doormat. One news reporter even managed to fry an egg under the building's rays. The solution was to add the metal "sunshade" you see today on the south of the building.

The Walkie Talkie is primarily an office block, but also houses restaurants and bars on the top floors, as well a public viewing gallery with one of the best free views of London. During the daytime free tickets are required from www.skygarden.london, but in the evening, the bar is open to the public without a ticket. The restaurants require reservations all day long.

Continue on Philpot Lane, cross over Fenchurch St., and head down Lime St. Turn left on Limestreet Passage and left again on Bull's Head Passage, part of Leadenhall Market.

If Leadenhall Market and these streets look like a film set, you would be right. In fact, just after number 42 Bull's Head Passage the building with a curved doorway was used as The Leaky Cauldron in Harry Potter and the Goblet of Fire – at the time of writing it is a beautician's shop.

Turn back onto Limestreet Passage, then left to the main covered area of Leadenhall Market (22).

Leadenhall Market was used in the first Potter film as the exterior location for Diagon Alley. However, the market dates back to 1321, when it sold meat.

The current market roof was designed in 1881 by Sir Horace Jones who is more famous for designing Tower Bridge. Jones also designed Billingsgate and Smithfield Markets which also still stand in The City. Leadenhall Market underwent a large refurbishment in the early 1990s.

22

Leadenhall Market is a joyful burst of colour in an otherwise grey, industrial and glass-filled area of London, and today mainly offers luxury clothing brands and dining.

Turn right down the market's main thoroughfare, passing the Lamb Tavern. As you exit the market, look up for Lloyd's of London (23), an unusual sight in The City,

Lloyd's of London, not to be confused with Lloyds Bank, is an insurance market in which insurers come together to spread risk and underwrite transactions.

23

The company was founded in 1686 in a coffeehouse owned by Edward Lloyd; the coffeehouse was the place to be in London to get shipping news and to obtain shipping insurance.

Over the years some unusual items have reportedly been insured under Lloyd's roof, including: Bruce Springsteen's voice, America Ferrara's smile (Ugly Betty), Gennaro Pelliccia's Tongue (chief coffee taster at Costa Coffee) and Mariah Carey's legs.

The first Lloyd's premises on the current site opened in 1928 – it soon outgrew this building and a second building was added in the 1950s. By the 1970s, Lloyd's had outgrown the two buildings and wanted a radical change so a design competition was started. Today's Lloyd's building is a result of that competition and was unveiled in 1986. It was designed by Richard Rogers and is now a protected 'listed' building. Historic England says the building is "universally recognised as one of the key buildings of the modern epoch".

The design style is called Bowellism in which the building's services such as the lifts, stairs and even pipes are on the outside of the building, therefore maximising interior space and making it easier to repair services from the outside if they ever become faulty.

Although most of the 1920s building was demolished, a large entranceway from the old building still stands on the other side of the current building on Leadenhall Street.

Continue to the corner of the Lloyd's Building and turn left onto Lime Street. Continue to the junction with Leadenhall Street. Now, you can either detour left to see the old entrance of Lloyd's of London, or stay on this corner to continue the tour.

Ahead, are two of the City's famous skyscrapers – The Gherkin (24) and The Cheesegrater (25).

The Gherkin is officially called 30 St Mary Axe and was completed in 2003. It stands 180 metres high and has 41 stories and is almost exclusively used as office space. The building was designed by Foster and Partners so that each floor is rotated by 5 degrees from that below it, resulting in the spiral pattern seen from the outside. The building's glass panels are all straight (not curved) apart from the one right at the top; the frame between the panels bends, not the glass.

The top three floors are bars and restaurants for the building's tenants, though public openings are often available with reservations. In 2014, the building was purchased for £700 million.

To the left of The Gherkin stands The Cheesegrater. Officially called The Leadenhall Building, it stands significantly taller than its aforementioned counterparts at 225m.

24

The building was designed by Rogers Stirk Harbour and Partners (who also designed the Lloyd's of London building). The Cheesegrater is a perfect example of the sight-lines to St. Paul's affecting the design of buildings in this area, as the building's design 'leans away' from the dome of St. Paul's when viewed from the west, including the view from Fleet Street. As with the other skyscrapers, this is an office building.

Between both buildings ahead is The Aviva Building, dating from the 1960s. It is to be demolished and replaced by a development called 1 Undershaft which will tower to 290 m and is due in the mid-to-late 2020s. It is set to be the tallest tower in The City when complete – for now.

To the right on the corner of Lime Street and Leadenhall Street is The Scalpel (26). In this case, this is the building's official name, like The Shard, and not just a nickname. The project was topped out in 2017 and is expected to be completed in 2018. It is 190 m tall, with 38 storeys and was designed by Kohn Pedersen Fox.

Amongst all these financial towers of glass stands a remnant of the old City. In the foreground of The Gherkin, is the magnificent St Andrew Undershaft (27) church.

St. Andrew's is not just a survivor of all the construction around it, it also incredibly survived both The Great Fire of London and The Blitz. The present church building was constructed in 1532, but a church has existed here since the 12th century. Even the organ is historic and dates from 1698. The church's style is called Perpendicular Gothic. The church's name stems from the shaft of the maypole that was traditionally set up each year opposite the church.

Turn right down Leadenhall Street. Soon on the left is St Katharine Cree (28) **church.**

This is another church which has survived all the change around it, though it suffered damage in The Blitz. The tower dates from about 1504, and the rest of the church was built between 1628 and 1630. Structural problems required extensive restoration in 1962. It is the only Jacobean era (early 17th century) church to survive in London. Despite the smoke-stained exterior, the inside is very colourful and worth seeing, including a beautiful 17th century original rose window.

Continue on Leadenhall Street. Where the road merges with Fenchurch Street to create Aldgate High Street look for the Aldgate Pump (29) **on the pavement to the right.**

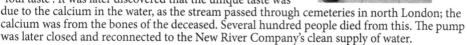

The Aldgate Pump was one of many pumps placed around London in the Victorian era which allowed easy access to drinking water. This particular one was erected here in 1876. However, a well has been located in this area since at least the 16th century and possibly as early as the 12th century.

The original pump was fed by one of London's many underground streams. Reports of the the water quality were mixed at the time: some praised it as "bright, sparkling, and cool, and of an agreeable taste", whereas others complained of a "foul taste". It was later discovered that the unique taste was due to the calcium in the water, as the stream passed through cemeteries in north London; the calcium was from the bones of the deceased. Several hundred people died from this. The pump was later closed and reconnected to the New River Company's clean supply of water.

The pump has a wolf head on it, supposedly as a marker for where the last wolf was shot in The City of London. The pump today no longer supplies water to the public.

Continue along Aldgate High Street on the right-hand pavement. On the corner of Jewry Street and Aldgate High Street is a blue plaque remembering this as the site of Aldgate (30).

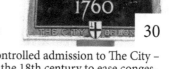

The historic Aldgate, which stood here until it was demolished in 1760, gives its name to the surrounding area today. Aldgate was the eastern-most entranceway through the London Wall. The meaning of the name Aldgate is unclear – it could mean "old gate", "ale gate" due to its proximity to an ale house, or even "all gate" as access to the gate was free to all.

London Wall and Aldgate were built by the Romans in the late 2nd or early 3rd century, likely as a defensive measure to keep enemies out of the city. The gate was rebuilt in the 12th century, 13th century and in the 17th century. Seven gates controlled admission to The City – the London Wall and most of the city gates were removed in the 18th century to ease congestion; today, none of the gates stand, although sections of the wall can be seen across the City.

Cross the street to the church on this other side.

This is St. Botolph without Aldgate (31) church – the "without" in the name means it was outside the London Wall. The current church dates from the 1740s and was designed by George Dance the Elder. It replaced a 16th century church which escaped the Great Fire of London. It is thought a church had existed on this site since at least the 12th century and possibly earlier.

Just after St. Botolph's church is Aldgate station where this tour ends.

Walk 9: Tower of London to Aldwych

Walk Length: 4.1 km / 2.6 mi
Timings: 1h 45m (fast), 2h 15m (regular), 2h 45m (leisurely)
Start: Tower Hill station
End: Temple station

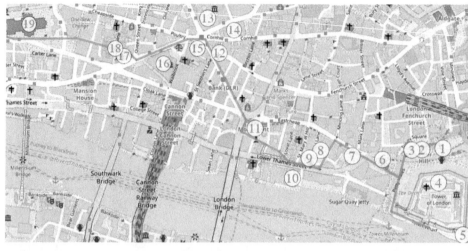

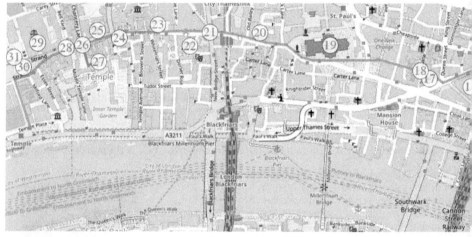

(1) London Wall	(17) Statue of a Cordwainer
(2) Trinity Square Gardens	(18) Bow Lane
(3) Tower Hill Scaffold	(19) St. Paul's Cathedral
(4) Tower of London	(20) St. Martin within Ludgate church
(5) Tower Bridge	(21) Ludgate Circus
(6) All Hallows by The Tower	(22) St. Bride's Church
(7) Hung, Drawn & Quartered Pub	(23) Ye Olde Cheshire Cheese
(8) St. Dunstan's in the East Church Garden	(24) El Vino
(9) Billingsgate Roman House & Baths	(25) St Dunstan in the West
(10) Old Billingsgate Fish Market	(26) Prince Henry's Room
(11) The Monument	(27) Temple Church
(12) St. Mary Woolnoth church	(28) Temple Bar Memorial
(13) Bank of England	(29) The Royal Courts of Justice
(14) Royal Exchange	(30) St. Clement Dane's church
(15) Mansion House	(31) Australian High Commission
(16) Bloomberg's London Office	

This tour begins at Tower Hill station. You can also start use the DLR to Tower Gateway and walk one minute to the Tower Hill station start point.

As you come out of Tower Hill station, turn left to see a fragment of the London Wall (1).

1

London Wall was built by the Romans in the late 2nd or early 3rd century, likely as a defensive measure to keep enemies out of the city. By the 7th century, London was a major Saxon port yet the wall had not been maintained and London suffered from two Viking attacks in the 9th century.

The wall was subsequently repaired, made taller and improved on during the 10th century, and again during the 11th century after the Norman Conquest of 1066. By this point the wall had accompanying ditches, towers, seven city gates for traffic, as well as pedestrian and water gates. The majority of the wall and the gates were removed in the 18th century to ease congestion in the city – this is one of the partial fragments of the wall can be seen throughout the City.

At the base of this magnificent historic wall is a statue of Roman emperor Trajan who ruled from 98 AD to 117AD, the time that the Romans were establishing the new city of Londinium. The statue has no date or sculptor attributed to it.

Head back past the station exit you just came through into the park called Trinity Square Gardens (2). **Head clockwise around the gardens.**

2

Ahead in the gardens you will come to a small building on your left and a dug-out memorial to your right. Collectively, the Tower Hill Memorial, remembers the sailors from the Merchant Navy and fishing fleets who died in the First and Second World Wars – as the inscription in the memorial says - "they have no grave but the sea."

The memorial to WWI was unveiled in 1928 by Queen Mary of Teck (Queen Elizabeth II's grandmother) and the WWII section in 1955 by Queen Elizabeth II. Feel free to explore the memorial in more detail if you wish.

Continue clockwise and soon on the right you will see a small square with chains around it.

These peaceful gardens were once the site of huge crowds of spectators and this specific square was the execution site of the Tower Hill scaffold (3). The scaffold was erected in 1485 for public executions and no fewer than 125 lost their lives here publically. Spectators would pay for the best view on the scaffold to watch the beheadings below, in an amphitheatre format.

3

Several well-known names are noted in the plaques in this spot, including:
• **St Thomas More** – More was councillor to King Henry VIII, who established the Church of England, yet he was an opponent to the Protestant Reformation and refused to acknowledge Henry as the Head of the Church and the King's marriage annulment to Catherine of Aragon. He was executed in 1535 for treason (betraying the country and king).
• **St John Fisher** – Fisher was a Cardinal and the Bishop of Rochester. Like More, Fisher refused to acknowledge Henry VIII as the Head of the Church of England and believed in Catholicism and the Pope's supremacy. He was also executed in 1535 under Henry's orders.
• **Thomas Cromwell** – Unlike the two men above, Cromwell was a chief minister of Henry VIII who strongly advocated for the English Reformation, assisting in the annulment of marriage to Catherine of Aragon and he even arranged Henry's fourth wife Anne of Cleves to be married to him. Cromwell had exaggerated Anne's beauty and when Henry found his bride

unattractive, Cromwell was imprisoned in the Tower of London and was executed in 1540 for treason and heresy (holding beliefs contrary to those commonly held).

Finally, the last man to be executed here has given us a very famous expression in the English language. This man was Simon Fraser, Lord Lovat – Fraser was sentenced to death as he encouraged his sons to join the Jacobite rebellion so that James II would rule. He was sentenced to death for high treason after a trial at Westminster Hall. On the day of his execution, the scaffold at Tower Hill became so overrun with spectators that it collapsed, killing nine people. Lord Lovat found this hilariously ironic and continued laughing until the axe came down, supposedly giving us the expression "laughing your head off".

Just outside the garden stands number 10 Trinity Square with its tall tower. This was the former headquarters of the Port of London Authority and this Beaux Arts-style building opened in 1922. Since 2017, the building has been used as a luxury hotel.

Exit to the south side of the gardens, crossing over the busy road onto the pedestrianised area with a magnificent view of the Tower of London (4)**.**

The story of the Tower of London goes back to 1066 when William the Conqueror invaded England at the Battle of Hastings. In 1078, work commenced on the Tower of London as a residence for King William I. The Tower has expanded to much more than the central White Tower with the 4 weather-vanes, and now encompasses an entire castle with two protective curtain walls.

The general layout we see today was finished in the late 13th century. A moat stands around the castle, although it has been drained and is today used to hold events throughout the year instead.

4

The Tower, as well as being used as a royal residence, has over time also been used as a prison (from 1100 up to WWII), a mint, an observatory and even a menagerie.

Henry VIII, our King from earlier in the walk, resided at the Tower of London and under his rule it underwent several refurbishments. Two of Henry's wives, Anne Boleyn and Catherine Howard were beheaded on the scaffold site inside the Tower under his orders. Another Queen of England, Lady Jane Grey was also beheaded here after reigning for only 9 days.

Today, the Yeoman Warders or "Beefeaters" live inside the Tower, guarding it and the Crown Jewels. Each of the Beefeaters (of which there are 37, plus one chief Warder) are former members of the Armed Forces, have served at least 22 years and hold the 'Long Service and Good Conduct' medal. The Beefeaters live with their families inside the Tower, though they must pay rent for their accommodation, some of which dates back to the 13th century. As well as guarding the Tower, since the Victorian era the Beefafters have given complimentary group tours of the castle which last about an hour and are well worth experiencing. No one knows exactly why there are called "Beefeaters", but the name may stem from the French phrase for the English – "les rosbifs" or "the roast beef eaters".

The other residents of the Tower of London are the famed ravens, large black birds. The legend says that if the ravens ever leave the tower, the Tower will crumble and the United Kingdom shall fall. Legend dictates that at least six of the birds should be kept at the Tower of London as tradition; to err on the safe side, there are eight of them – in addition, their lifting feathers have been clipped to stop them from flying too far. The birds are known for being extremely intelligent and you will no doubt see a few guarding the Tower and flying around during your visit. A Raven Master takes care of the ravens and feeds them their daily ration of 170g of raw meat and blood-soaked biscuits.

One of the most famous reasons for visiting the Tower of London is to see The Crown Jewels. The original Crown Jewels were destroyed in 1649 when Oliver Cromwell overthrew the monarchy and beheaded King Charles I; in this process, he had the jewels destroyed. Only one item survives from before 1649, which is the Coronation Spoon dating back to the 12th century used during the anointing of the monarch in the coronation ceremony. Upon the re-establishing of the monarchy in 1660, Charles II had new Crown Jewels created, and subsequent monarchs have added to the collection.

Notable parts of the Crown Jewels include: the ceremonial maces often see in Parliament, the Sword of Offering, the gold-thread Imperial Mantle, the Coronation Ring, St. Edward's Crown (only used during coronation) dating back to 1660, the Sovereign's orb, and the Sovereign's Sceptre with Cross which features the Cullinan I diamond - the largest cut colourless diamond in the world, weighing in at 530.2 carats. That is not to mention the banqueting plates, altar collection, and of course the Imperial State Crown – the crown the queen uses during ceremonies today. In total there are over 140 objects in this truly magnificent collection and they are the must-see sight in London in our opinion.

Officially, the Crown Jewels are priceless and therefore they are not insured, however estimates of between £3-5 billion are often cited. The Cullinan I diamond alone is estimated to be worth at least £400 million.

If you plan on going inside the Tower of London, allow a minimum of 3 to 4 hours to see the Crown Jewels, do a Beefeater tour and have a look around at the various exhibits.

Continue down the ramp with the Tower of London to your left until you reach the River Thames at the bottom, and have a magnificent view of Tower Bridge (5).

Tower Bridge, often incorrectly called London Bridge, has stood on its current site since 1894. Designed by Horace Jones, its aim was to reduce traffic on the next bridge to the west called London Bridge.

The area that you are standing in today was previously known as the Pool of London and was, at the time, an integral part of the largest port in the world. As such, ships needed to be able to pass through the proposed location of Tower Bridge – several designs were proposed including some with long access routes but the winning design was the once we see today. The level with the traffic crossing features two bascules (or drawbridges) in the centre which raise up when necessary to allow ships through to this area between Tower Bridge and London Bridge. The whole process usually results in a pausing of traffic of about 8 minutes.

Tower Bridge was designed with the two central towers and the raised walkway to allow people crossing the bridge on foot to continue to cross even when the bascules were raised, by using a lift to get to the top, going across the walkway and coming back down the other side. After a surge in crime on the top walkways, including a huge amount of prostitution and theft, the walkways were closed to the public. Today they are accessible as part of the paid-admission Tower Bridge exhibition.

Despite the Cornish granite-look of the bridge, the frame and supports are in fact made of 11,000 tons of steel. The stonework is only cladding to decorate the bridge, so it fits in with the Tower of London: after all, the Tower of London dates from 800 years before the bridge.

Bridge lifts are a constant source of annoyance for road passengers today and cause a substantial increase in traffic when they happen. Today, the process is strictly controlled with traffic lights, an audible alarm and gates closing before the bridge lifts begin.

Previously, though, the process was more manual, and relied more heavily on personnel to do the job correctly. Due to a lapse in judgement, in December 1952, the bridge bascules began to raise with a double-decker bus still on one of the bascules – the driver took a brave decision and accelerated at maximum speed and jumped the gap between the bascules. London is the home of James Bond after all!

Across the river, the curved modern building is City Hall, the headquarters of the Greater London Council and where the Mayor of London works with 32 London boroughs to acheive city-wide aims. The building was designed by Norman Foster and was completed in 2002 – it was the start of a large regeneration of the area across the river, which today is known as "More London" but was previously a series of wharves serving the Pool of London.

City Hall has been nicknamed "the motorcycle helmet" and "the leaning tower of pizzas" in the past. The glass design and helix staircase inside supposedly symbolise the transparency of government.

The large blue warship across the river is H.M.S. Belfast, completed in 1939 and used by the Royal Navy at the D-Day Landings in Normandy during WWII. The guns at the front could fire a shell at a distance of 23 km if necessary. Since 1971 the ship has been moored here permanently and it is now an excellent museum.

Also across the river is The Shard, which is spoken about in more detail on Walk 8. The Shard is Western Europe's tallest skyscraper standing at 1016 feet tall and is designed to look like a shard of glass – it was inaugurated in 2012.

Retrace your steps up alongside the Tower of London. Turn left to the church with a green spire.

6

All Hallows by the Tower (6) is the oldest church still standing in the City of London, dating back to 675. The original church was rebuilt many times between the 11th and 15th centuries. In the 17th century, it was badly damaged by an explosion, but it survived the Great Fire of London; diarist Samuel Pepys climbed the spire to write about the devastation in The City during the Fire. The church was then rebuilt in the Victorian era, only to be destroyed by a bomb during The Blitz; it was only rededicated in 1957.

The church is, therefore, almost like a time capsule with different parts surviving from different eras, including one archway inside from the original church from 675. It is worth going inside and visiting the free Crypt Museum where you can see remains of a Roman building and pavement which were on this site before the church's construction, as well as original documents, other artefacts and the subterranean chapels. It is a real hidden gem and worth spending a few minutes walking around.

The church also has a few American connections: William Penn, who went on to found Pennsylvania and was key in the Quaker movement, was baptised here; and John Quincy Adams (6th US president) was married at the church.

Continue ahead across Byward Street and stop by the Hung, Drawn and Quartered Pub (7).

The pub itself is not particularly historic, nor are we interested in the building – we care about its name. The pub's name remembers a form of public execution which used to place on Tower Hill where we began our tour. Being "hanged, drawn and quartered" was the common punishment for high treason and was the country's most extreme form of capital punishment – the first recorded use of it was in the 13th century.

(Those with a nervous disposition should skip this next explanation.)

The process was as follows:
1) Hanged - A public hanging with a noose almost until the point of death
2) Drawn - Organs are removed through an incision in the abdominal area, followed or preceeded by a beheading

3) Quartered - Cut into four pieces either with swords/axes, or using four horses attached to the four main limbs to rip the body apart.

A plaque on the side of the building with a quote from Samuel Pepys says: "I went to see Major General Harrison Hung, Drawn and Quartered. He was looking as cheerful as any man could in that condition." In 1649 General Harrison signed the death warrant which led to the execution of Charles I; upon the restoration of the monarchy in 1660, Harrison was found guilty of regicide and executed by being hanged, drawn and quartered.

Continue down Great Tower Street to the right of the pub. Take the first left down St. Dunstan's Hill and enter the unusual St. Dunstan's in the East Church Garden (8).

The first St. Dunstan's in the East church was built on this site at the start of the 12th century. The church was severely damaged in the Great Fire of London in 1666. Instead of fully rebuilding the church, much like All Hallows which we saw a few minute's ago, this church was repaired and famed architect Christopher Wren added the new steeple in a gothic style. In the 19th century it was found that the older parts of the church were not structurally sound and these were rebuilt, with the steeple maintained. However, then came The Blitz air raids in WWII which severely damaged the church – the tower survived, as did the fragments of walls around you.

8

The City of London decided that instead of rebuilding the church yet again, this space could be converted into a public garden with carefully cared for plants designed to look like they are overrunning the walls. This is an excellent stop to relax for a few minutes and it is amazing how serene it is despite being surrounded by major roads just a few feet away. Today the ruin is a grade I listed structure and you will very often see photoshoots and even wedding receptions here, and on weekdays at lunchtime in the warmer months, you will see office workers enjoying some well needed peace and lunch.

Exit out the south side of the garden and head downhill to the busy Lower Thames Street. Turn right (west) and stop by the first door to your right marked number 101.

Underneath this mundane-looking Queen Elizabeth House building is the site of the Billingsgate Roman House & Baths (9), which dates back to the creation of London 2000 years ago. Amazingly it has survived the Great Fire, The Blitz and being rebuilt on countless times. The site was discovered in 1848 when the Coal Exchange was built on this site.

The ruins are believed to be "a modest bath house preserved within the courtyard of a much larger structure, possibly an inn". The house would likely also have been on the waterfront of the Thames when the river was much wider.

When the Coal Exchange was replaced with the current building in the 1970s, the ruins were preserved in the basements as a condition of granting planning permission. Today, the site is accessible to the public through guided tours only on a few selected days each year – details can be obtained at bit.ly/romanbathhouse.

Continue west along Lower Thames Street. Shortly on the other side of the road you will see a building with several archways, Old Billingsgate Fish Market (10).

10

The Billingsgate Fish Market was started next to the River Thames informally in the 16th century and was officially established in 1699. In 1850, the current building was constructed to replace the collection of sheds from individual traders, and an extension was added in 1874-7 by Sir Horace Jones (the architect of Tower Bridge fame).

The original building was designed by J. B. Bunning, the City architect at the time. This was the booming time for central London's fish trade and in the 19th century this building housed what is believed to be the largest fish market in the world at the time.

In 1982, the market relocated to east London near Canary Wharf where it still trades to this day. This reflects the change in how fish arrives in London, from the river, to the railways and today by road. Today, this building is used as a conference and events venue.

Bear right up Monument Street towards The Monument (11), **the 202-foot tall column which remembers the Great Fire of 1666. We cover this topic in a lot more detail in Walk 8, so do feel free to refer to this walk if you wish.**

Continue past The Monument until you are on King William Street. Turn right, pass Monument station. Follow the map across the junction onto King William Street. This road was built between 1829 and 1835 and is named after the monarch at the time, William IV.

Up ahead, before the major intersection look out for St. Mary Woolnoth church (12) on the right hand side. Incredibly, this very site has been built on for religious purposes since the Romans arrived and established London almost 2,000 years ago.

The current church building dates from 1727 and was designed by Nicholas Hawkmoor (famous for the west towers of Westminster Abbey – the most recognisable side). This church was created under the orders of the Commission for Building Fifty New Churches, which aimed to built fifty new churches for the city's rapidly expanding population – only a fraction of those were built. This is the only church by Nicholas Hawksmoor in the City of London. The church still conducts services to this day and is heavily used by city's Swiss community.

Continue ahead and you will reach the large Bank junction.

The tall, wide building on the opposite side of this junction is the Bank of England (13) with its curtained wall with no windows. This institution is also known as "the old lady of Threadneedle Street" due to how long it has been here and gives this area and the station underground its name, Bank.

The Bank of England was founded on 27th July 1694 as the banker to the government, primarily to fund the war against France at the time. King William III at the time stated the Bank's aim as to "promote the public Good and Benefit of our People". When it opened the following month, the Bank only had 19 members of staff. In the same year, the bank began accepting deposits from the public and acted much like any other bank would today. The first printed banknotes were issued by the Bank in 1725: before then, they were all hand-written.

12

The Bank moved to its current location in 1734 in a Palladian-style building designed by George Sampson, and over the next century the Bank bought up all the properties surrounding it until it had land totalling 3.5 acres. Sir John Soane was the architect who began to extend Bank to its current size in the 1780s, and added the curtain wall in 1828 – crucially, for security reasons, no buildings adjoin the Bank on any side.

Soane's building was demolished and it was replaced by the current building between 1925 and 1939 and was designed by Sir Herbert Baker– the new building is 10 stories in height (including 3 under ground), whereas the old building was only 3 stories at its highest point. Soane's outer wall still stands surrounding the modern building. The Bank was nationalised just a few years later in 1946. By 1997, it was made independent, though it is still owned by the Government.

13

Today the Bank of England has four main responsibilities: regulating other banks, issuing and printing bank notes (of which there are 3 billion in circulation), setting monetary policy such the UK's interest rate; and maintaining stability by making sure the financial system is safe and operating correctly. The Bank today does not hold accounts or offer loans to the public.

If you want to find out more about the bank's current role and its history, there is an excellent free admission museum open on weekdays inside the bank – the entrance the museum is on Bartholomew Lane.

On the east side of the intersection (to the right) is the Royal Exchange (14).

The Royal Exchange was founded by Thomas Gresham in 1571, and was unveiled by Queen Elizabeth I. The building's purpose was to allow a centralised place for exchanges to take place; stockbrokers were not allowed due to their brusque nature. The original building burnt down in the Great Fire in 1666, its replacement was used by Lloyd's insurance but also also burnt down in 1838. The current building dates from 1844 and was designed by William Tite to resemble the original building – it was unveiled by Queen Victoria.

14

The frieze at the top of the building features Commerce in the centre and an inscription in Latin below telling us about the opening and restoration of the Royal Exchange by the two aforementioned monarchs. You may also be able to spot a weather vane of a golden grasshopper on top – this is part of the Gresham family crest.

Today the Royal Exchange is used as a shopping centre with a bar in the centre and is well worth looking inside – there are also free toilets. The Royal Exchange is open Monday to Friday during standard business hours.

On the western side of this major junction is a building which is not look too dissimilar to the Royal Exchange. This is Mansion House (15), the official residence of the Lord Mayor of the City of London.

It is worth pointing out that this a separate person and job to the Mayor of London based in City Hall, which we saw earlier in the walk. The Lord Mayor is only responsible for The City (the financial district), whereas the Mayor of London is responsible for Greater London and has more powers. The Lord Mayor's main role nowadays is to represent, support and promote the businesses and residents of the City of London, and also fulfil ceremonial duties - the term only lasts one year.

15

The first recorded Mayor of London was Henry Fitz-Ailwyn in 1189. As of January 2018, the current serving Mayor is number 690.

The building dates from 1752 and was designed by George Dance the Elder in the Palladian style, though it has undergone major remodelling since then. The building is still used as the Lord Mayor's official residence and for The City's official functions, including two white tie dinners each year: at Easter the Foreign Secretary speaks, and in June the Chancellor of the Exchequer makes a speech.

Underneath all this is one of London's busiest tube stations, Bank, opened in 1900. If you ever ride the central line from the east into this station you will hear a lot of wheel squeal as the trains are forced around sharp bends in the tunnels put in place by the railway company to avoid the vaults of the Bank of England.

Walk past Mansion House and continue along Queen Victoria Street.

The modern building on the left which runs along this street after the Magistrates' court is Bloomberg's London office (16), opened in October 2017. Designed at a cost of £1 billion by Foster and Partners, the building was given the accolade of being the most sustainable major office development ever constructed anywhere in the world, with a score of 98.5%.

16

The site of this building was home to the Temple of Mithras dating from the mid-3rd century and likely built by the Romans. The Temple was discovered during construction of the building which previously occupied this spot in 1954 and was moved 100m to the west and made into an outdoor display visible at no charge.

As part of the development of the Bloomberg building project, the Temple was relocated back to a spot very close to its original location 7 m (23 ft) underground and is now part of a free museum called the London Mithraeum which is funded by Bloomberg. The museum uses an excellent light and sound show to reveal the ruins in a dramatic fashion and is worth a visit. At busy times, you may need to book a slot to enter. To find it, turn left after the Magistrates Court onto Bucklersbury, then right onto Walbrook – the museum is to your right.

Continue along Queen Victoria Street, bearing right onto Watling Street to the right of St. Mary Aldermary, dating from 1681 and designed by Christopher Wren.

Immediately behind the church is a statue of a Cordwainer (17), an old word for a shoemaker, as this was the centre of the shoemaking industry in London. The word stems from the town of Córdoba in Andalusia, Spain where leather was made – this leather was brought back by The Crusaders and was used in high quality footwear. The Cordwainer statue, by Alma Boyes, was unveiled in 2002 to celebrate the centenary of the Ward of Cordwainer Club.

Continue to the corner with Ye Olde Watling pub and Bow Lane (18) **running across.**

This is our first example of a classic old City of London street as it would have been in the 16th and 17th century. All the buildings date from more recent times, but it is the width and layout of the streets that are important to us.

In the 15th, 16th and 17th centuries the buildings around you would have been tenements and much taller with some reaching 8 or 9 floors in height. The upper floors of the buildings were built using a technique called "jettying" - the higher up they went, the more the floors stuck out over the road – this maximised the floor space in the upper floors, while still allowing space for a street to exist at ground level. The buildings would have been made mostly of wood and incredibly overcrowded. London's population in the mid-1660s was between 400,000 and 500,000 people, and by far the biggest city in the country and one of the largest in the world.

Very little sunlight would make it down to the streets and there was no sanitation system – the streets were open sewers. Residents would use go to the toilet in chamber pots in their houses and when these were full they would throw the human waste from the upper floors down into the street. The streets were filled with human, household and animal waste. The City of London employed 'rakers' who would attempt to clean the streets, although they were ineffective. The only thing that did clear the streets, however, was rain – when it rained, the streets would floor and the waste would descend downhill, usually ending up in the River Thames which was an enormous open sewer for the whole city.

Diseases were common and the city had very basic medical services, and poverty was rife throughout the city. Much earlier, in 1348, England suffered from a disease known as the Black Death – the lack of records make it difficult to estimate, but historians today believe that between 25% and 60% of the entire country's population was killed by the disease.

The bubonic plague struck the city on several occasions including in 1603, 1625 and 1636 – these three incidences led to deaths totalling 75,000 people. London suffered almost 40 large-scale disease outbreaks between 1348 and 1665.

London experienced The Great Plague in 1665. The Plague was spread by the rats moving along the streets and inside buildings; the rats would became infested by fleas and if these fleas jumped onto a human, they would spread the plague. 60–80% of those who caught The Plague died, and most of those died within a week. Some of the symptoms of the plague included boils called bubos (hence the "bubonic plague") growing on the skin, fever and vomiting of blood. In just 18 months, almost a quarter of London's population was killed by the Great Plague. This was the last widespread outbreak of the Plague in the city.

The Plague subsided in the colder months and in February 1666, King Charles II returned to the city. Some believe the Great Fire of London in 1666 killed off the final strands of the disease, thereby ending the Plague in the city.

Continue down Watling Street with a view of Christopher Wren's St. Paul's Cathedral (19)**, built between 1675 and 1710. The cathedral is covered in more detail on Walk 8.**

Walk towards the Cathedral and follow the road to the left of the church. Pass the modern City of London information centre across the road, until you are at the main entrance of the church with the flights of steps.

With St. Paul's on the right, head down Ludgate Hill and you shortly reach St. Martin within Ludgate church (20)**.**

19

St. Martin within Ludgate is a Christopher Wren-designed church that was built between 1677-84 after The Great Fire. The "within" in the name of the church tells us that the Church was within the City Walls.

A blue plaque towards the left side of the church remembers the City gate which used to stand here – gate Lud, hence "Ludgate Hill" being the name of the road. Lud is unlikely to have any connection to King Lud, and is more likely to come from "flood gate" as this gate was on a bridge over the River Fleet which flowed at the bottom of the hill (and still does today – but underground). The gate was demolished in 1760 along with the other City gates.

Head down Ludgate Hill to Ludgate Circus (21)**, a major road junction.**

The 'circus' in the crossing's name means 'circle', and the buildings on each corner of the crossing resemble a circle from the air.

Farringdon Street to the right follows the path of the River Fleet. Today the boats have been replaced by cars, pedestrians and London's fastest growing form of transport, the bicycle. Along this road is a segregated portion of the impressively wide Cycle Superhighway 6. The first of these major bike paths was announced by Mayor of London Ken Livingstone in 2008. Successive Mayors have continued this trend, with current mayor Sadiq Khan making major a commitment of £770 million over his 4-year term to new bike infrastructure. London also runs a Cycle Hire scheme accessible to both locals and visitors – you have no doubt spotted some of these bikes dotted around the city.

Cross over Ludgate Circus onto Fleet Street ahead.

Fleet Street is synonymous in the UK with the newspaper industry and was once known as "the street of ink". Indeed, the first daily newspaper in the world, the Daily Courant, was published in a building on Ludgate Circus in 1702. Newspapers in the 18th century were expensive and most people could not read, so their appeal was limited.

However, with the rise in education and the repeal of the newspaper tax in 1855, newspapers became the new must-have accessory in Victorian London. Coffeehouses stocked newspapers and were the place to be seen in the city. Fleet Street became a hub of activity with all major newspapers being written and printed on this street.

By the 1980s, the cost of newspaper production was too high to be done in such a central location. The advent of satellite technology and the internet made it possible to have newspapers produced in any location and printed off-site anywhere else. Today, the newspaper industry has all but disappeared from the street.

22

Shortly on the right, the black, modern building with Express in red letters at number 120 is the old Daily Express building, which despite its modern look was built between 1930 and 1932 – the Express newspapers are no longer based here.

Across the street, the stone building is number 85 – home to Metro International, perhaps the only major publishing company still based on the street.

23

Look down St. Bride's Avenue to the left of number 85 for a view of St. Bride's Church (22), another Christopher Wren masterpiece dating from 1672.

It is said that the modern day tiered wedding cake is based on the design of this church. The story goes that in 1703 Thomas Rich, a baker's apprentice from Ludgate Hill, fell in love with his employer's daughter and asked her to marry him. He wanted a wedding cake unlike any other and therefore based it on the design of St Bride's Church.

A few doors further along is a colourful clock from the upper floors of an Egyptian-style art deco building from 1920. This is number 135-141 Fleet Street, and was home to the Daily Telegraph until the 1980s. Today, both this and the Express building are offices of Goldman Sachs.

Almost immediately after the Telegraph Building, look for the black pub with a lantern outside called Ye Olde Cheshire Cheese (23), one of the most atmospheric pubs in London.

The current building dates from 1667, though there has been a pub here since 1538. You can enjoy a drink on the ground floor or use the low stairs to descend further inside.

The vaults cellars are thought to have been past of a 13th-century monastery which once occupied the site – today these same cellars make for great drinking spaces. Regular patrons of the pub included Charles Dickens, Mark Twain, Sir Arthur Conan Doyle and Alfred Tennyson.

Be sure to step inside if it is open, even if you do not stop for a drink. The pub also serves food. Opening hours are 11:30am to 11:00pm from Monday to Saturday. Closed on Sundays.

Further up Fleet Street, on the other side of the road stands the Tipperary, the first pub outside of Ireland to serve Guinness – initially bottled, and then on draft.

Continue along Fleet Street and cross to the other side of the road at Fetter Lane.

Note El Vino (24), one of the city's most well-know wine merchants and bars which dates back to 1879. Frank Bower, the man who started the company, developed the 'house rule' of never selling a wine he did not consider ready to drink.

Continue along Fleet Street.

Soon on the right hand side you will see the tower and clock of St Dunstan in the West (25). The current church building dates from 1830 and was designed by John Shaw, though a church has exited on the site since the 10th or 11th century. The previous church was not destroyed in the Great Fire, but rather it was to widen the road in the 19th century.

The clock next to the tower has figures, possibly Gog and Magog – mentioned in the Bible and Hebrew scriptures, which strike the bell with their clubs every hour. The clock face underneath them was also the first in London to have a minute hand. The clock dates from 1671.

The white building to the left of this church (with its own clock) is 186 Fleet Street, which was the site of Sweeney Todd's barber shop. Sweeney Todd is a well-known fiction-al character, most recently popularised by the 2007 film

25

Sweeney Todd: The Demon Barber of Fleet Street featuring Johnny Depp and Helena Bonham Carter. In the story, Sweeney Todd would lead would-be victims inside his barber shop, slicing their throats with his shaving blade, and grinding them into mince meat before his accom-plice and lover Ms. Lovett bakes them into pies and sells them at her pie shop to unsuspecting customers.

The story does not appear to have any basis in truth but none-the-less lives on in musicals, films and our minds over 150 years after the character first appeared in The String of Pearls written by James Malcolm Rymer and/or Thomas Peckett Prest as a serialised story.

Ahead, on the left side of the road, at number 22 is Ye Olde Cock Tavern. Perhaps the narrow-est pub façade in London, this pub was rebuilt in the 1880s (and restored in the 1990s after a fire) but its origins date back to 1549 when it was originally located on the other side of the road until it was demolished to make way for a branch of the Bank of England (seen shortly).

A few doors further down at number 17 is the black and white wooden building known as Prince Henry's Room (26).

This building is a rare example of a building which survived the Great Fire of London. It dates from 1610 and still has much of its original timber frame. The building has been a pub, a waxwork museum, and a museum to Samuel Pepys over the years; it is not open to the public.

26

Under this building is a gate which may be open during your visit – usually on weekdays until 8:30pm, though it sporadically opens and closes. If it is open, proceed inside into Inner and Middle Temple, part of The City's law dis-trict. If not, skip the next section.

At the end of this small alleyway is Temple Church (27), which dates from 1185 when the Knight's Templar, cru-sading monks founded to protect pilgrims on their way to and from Jerusalem, founded a temple here. The Church is generally open on Mon, Tues, Thurs and Fri, 10am-4pm and 2pm-4pm on Wednesdays and is well worth a visit, particu-larly for anyone who has read or watched Dan Brown's 'The Da Vinci Code' in which the church features heavily.

Back on Fleet Street, continue ahead.

You will pass The Old Bank of English on your right, once a branch of the central Bank and today a pub.

In the centre of the road ahead is the Temple Bar Memorial (28) which replaced the gatehouse which stood here in 1878.

Temple Bar now stands near St Paul's Cathedral (see it on Walk 8). This memorial dates from 1880, and features a dragon on top. On the sides of the memorial are Queen Victoria and her son Edward, the last royals to have entered through the gate that once stood here. Today this is also the boundary between The City of London and The City of Westminster. The street from here onwards is called Strand.

The beautiful building across the street is The Royal Courts of Justice (29).

Despite its gothic church-like façade, this building was only built in the 1870s and unveiled in 1882 by Queen Victoria. It is therefore of a Gothic revival style and it was purpose-designed as a court of law. The majority of the building is red-brick; the stone is only used on the Fleet street façade and in the main interior hall.

The building houses the High Court and Court of Appeal of England and Wales, high up the judicial system; any appeals of decisions made in these courts are directed to the highest court in the land, the Supreme Court, on Parliament Square.

The courts are open to the public at no charge, so on weekdays you can go through security and enter the building and you can explore the maze of 1,000 rooms and corridors – if you have a few minutes to spare, we highly recommend it.

On the left side of the road ahead by the pedestrian crossing to the Royal Courts of Justice is Twinings. Thomas Twining opened Britain's first known tea room at No. 216 Strand, in 1706; it still operates today. This shop is therefore London's longest-standing ratepayer, having never moved premises since opening. Twinings also has the world's oldest continually-used company logo. Twinings has been a holder of a Royal Warrant and supplied tea to the Royal Household since Queen Victoria appointed the company this honour in 1837.

Looking up at the Twinings building, you can see how shoups would have been in the early 18th century – deep, but certainly not tall. The shop has not filled the void above its building created by the newer establishments to its left and right.

Continue ahead using the pavement to go round the left of the church in the centre of Strand ahead.

This is St. Clement Danes church (30), designed in 1682 by Christopher Wren. The church was, however, gutted during The Blitz and only restored in the 1950s, with much of the shrapnel damage kept intact – particularly on the other side. Today it is the official church of the Royal Air Force. Its bells also chime the melody from the nursery rhyme "Oranges and Lemons Sing the Bells of St. Clement's".

Once round the church the roads widen significantly. Look for the building with the green roof in the centre of the two major roads ahead – this is the Australian High Commission (31).

A High Commission serves much the same function as an embassy but the title is reserved for countries which are part of the Commonwealth of Nations. Australia House's construction began in 1913 and completed in 1918 when it was unveiled by George V. The building was designed by Scotsman Alexander Marshall Mackenzie and his son, Alexander George Robertson Mackenzie. Much of the building materials were imported from Australia.

Harry Potter fans will be wishing they could get inside as the interior of Gringotts Bank was filmed here for Harry Potter and the Philosopher's Stone.

Here ends our tour. The nearest tube station is Temple, just two minutes away. Turn left down Arundel Street and walk down the hill to reach the station.

Walk 10: Camden, Regent's Park and Baker Street

Walk Length: 4.0 km / 2.5 mi
Timings: 2h (fast), 2h 30m (regular), 3h (leisurely)
Start: Chalk Farm station
End: Baker Street station

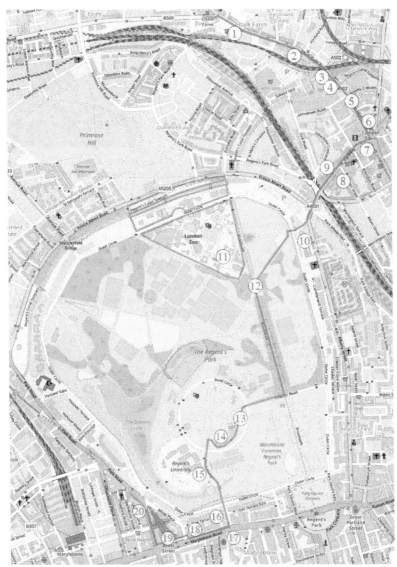

(1) The Roundhouse	(11) London Zoo
(2) Stables Market	(12) Ready Money Drinking Fountain
(3) Camden Lock Market	(13) Queen Mary's Rose Gardens
(4) Regent's Canal	(14) Japanese Garden
(5) Camden High Street	(15) Regents University London
(6) Electric Ballroom	(16) Properties on York Terrace
(7) Jazz Café	(17) St. Marylebone Church
(8) Jewish Museum	(18) Madame Tussauds
(9) The Dublin Castle pub	(19) Sherlock Holmes Statue
(10) Properties on Gloucester Gate	(20) Sherlock Holmes Museum

95

This tour begins at Chalk Farm station.

The name of Chalk Farm station and the surrounding area derives from the area's historic name of "Chaldecot" meaning a "cold cottage" or "cold shelter". It is thought the area was used heavily as a resting spot for people travelling into the city. It does not, in fact, appear that there was a specific farm here that the area was named after. The area began to become urbanised when nearby Camden Town was built up as a residential district in the 1790s.

Turn left out of the tube station on Adelaide Road and then right onto Havestock Hill/Chalk Farm Road. Be sure to be on the right-hand-side pavement. Shortly on your right you will see The Roundhouse (1).

The urbanisation of Chalk Farm and Camden Town was rapid in the 1800s as the area's water canal system was built in the 1810s, followed by the arrival of railways shortly thereafter.

The Roundhouse was built as a railway shed in 1847 by the London and North Western railway; it contained a turntable and space for train repairs. The Roundhouse was only used for this purpose for a decade, before it was converted into a warehouse and used for about 70 years before being abandoned in the 1930s.

In 1964, the building was converted into a theatre and performance venue by playwright Arnold Wesker. The building once again fell into disuse by the 1980s and was reopened in 2006 as the arts venue you see today. The Roundhouse was famously used by Apple's free iTunes Festival between 2011 and 2014 with performances from Lady Gaga, Ed Sheeran, Linkin' Park and Status Quo amongst many others.

Continue along Chalk Farm Road, passing the petrol station and soon a tall wall appears on the right hand side. Head along the left side of this wall (still on Chalk Farm Road) until you reach the entrance of Stables Market (2).

This is the first of six markets which join together to form the Camden markets – we will pass two on this tour. Do feel free to explore these individually while on this walk.

Stables Market was founded in the 19th century as a network of stable blocks, workshops and tunnels, with a large horse hospital. The stables here held over 400 horses in 1925. By the 1940s, this area was fully industrialised with the major train stations of Kings Cross and St Pancras just over a mile away; horses would help pull trains along the tracks, and river barges along the canal. By the 1940s around 800 horses worked at the enormous Camden Goods Depot hence the need for these stables.

Today, there are no horses but lots of shopping opportunities instead – chain stores are not allowed inside the market and the focus is on handmade goods, second-hand items, antiques and household decorations. If you decide to go inside, look out for the statue of Amy Winehouse (who lived nearby at 30 Camden Square – a 20-minute walk away from our route) and for the unusual shop Cyberdog straight ahead which describes itself as stocking "futuristic fashion, rave outfits, and cyber club wear. Born in the 90's, worn in the future."

Continue along Chalk Farm Road.

Look out for number 19 on the left with a giant chair outside. Large objects outside shops like this are a common way of grabbing your attention in Camden enticing you to shop there, and you will see plenty more of these.

Pass under the railway bridge ahead and the first turning on the right is the entrance to Camden Lock Market (3). **Look back at the railways bridge for a classic photo with the market's name.**

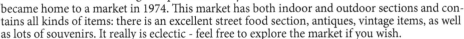
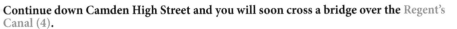

3

Camden Lock Market's site was originally warehouses for the shipping and rail trade.

However, as both these industries became mechanised the warehouses were no longer required and they became home to a market in 1974. This market has both indoor and outdoor sections and contains all kinds of items: there is an excellent street food section, antiques, vintage items, as well as lots of souvenirs. It really is eclectic - feel free to explore the market if you wish.

Continue down Camden High Street and you will soon cross a bridge over the Regent's Canal (4)**.**

The Regent's Canal began construction in 1812 and by 1820 the entire 8.6-mile (13.8-km) canal was complete. It begins at Paddington where it joins the Grand Union Canal, cuts through north London and eventually ends in East London at Limehouse.

The naming of Regent's Canal comes from the fact it was one of many major projects completed under the rule of George Frederick while he was acting as regent on behalf of his father George III, before later reigning as George IV.

This period is called the Regency. Hence the names of Regent Street, Regent's Park and the Regent's Canal, for example. John Nash was the architect commissioned to work on the project, though much of the design work was actually done by James Morgan.

The purpose of the canal was to move cargo arriving by ship at London's ports to the Midlands and vice-versa. When steam trains were popularised and seen as a cheaper and more efficient way of moving goods, the canals fell out of use. Today they are mainly used for recreational purposes.

You can catch a waterbus or canal boat from the canal area to the right on weekends in winter and daily in summer. Several trips are run each day and a 50-minute trip from Camden Lock Market will take you through London Zoo and then towards Little Venice – prices are £9 per adult and £7.50 per child in 2018; no cash – card only. See londonwaterbus.com for the timetable.

Continue along Camden High Street (5)**, which is almost always incredibly busy, until you reach Camden Town station.**

As you walk along the street you will likely notice that Camden is unlike most other well-known areas of London. It has a certain gritty feel to it, it is not as sterilised and it may even feel more real that the likes of Mayfair and Knightsbridge.

Camden has been home of London's alternative culture since at least the 1970s, and many would argue that the 'punk' scene began here – at The Roundhouse, in fact, and at Dingwalls (a venue inside Camden Lock Market). Here, The Ramones played, inspiring The Clash, The Sex Pistols and many others.

Camden became the centre of London and Britain's music scene thereafter with House music appearing in the 1980s, Brit Pop in the 1990s and in the 2000s it was where The Libertines, Amy Winehouse and others played. Camden is still one of London's nightlife hotspots. Unfortunately, due to gentrification the artists that once lived in the area are being pushed out and Camden has certainly changed over the past decade as the luxury flats and hipster coffee shops have arrived.

Walk along Camden High Street. Just before Camden Town station, look out for the Electric Ballroom (6) **on the left side of the road.**

The Electric Ballroom is one of London's most iconic venues and has stood here in one form or another since 1938. In the 1970s, The Clash rehearsed here, as did Paul McCartney's Wings, Led Zeppelin and Gary Glitter. The '80s saw The Cramps, The Fall, U2 and The Smiths play here, amongst others. More recently Snow Patrol, The Kings of Leon and Alt-J have performed at the venue.

At the junction with Camden Town Station, turn right down Parkway. Stay on the right-hand pavement.

Another of Camden's music venues soon appears on the left – the Jazz Café (7), which appeared on the scene in Camden in 1990. It is unique in that it works both as a performance venue and as a restaurant. Amy Winehouse, Pharaoh Sanders and Eddie Harris are just some of the artists who have performed here over the years.

Parkway is a good example of the gentrified side of Camden with its coffee shops, gastro-pubs and boutiques, mixing in with some of the older music-focused establishments and shops of the area.

Continue ahead along Parkway. For reference, on Albert Street to the left is the excellent Jewish Museum (8) which tells the story of Britain's Jewish communities. There is a charge for entry. On this tour we continue along Parkway.

Number 94 Parkway on the right is home to the red and white The Dublin Castle pub (9).

9

When the railway and canal industries took off in the area, workers from all around the British Isles came to work here. The different communities didn't get along well and fights and brawls were common, so each community had its own pub: The Dublin Castle, The Edinburgh Castle, The Pembroke Castle and The Warwick Castle.

The band, The Madness started at the Dublin Castle in 1979, and Amy Winehouse worked at the pub in her early singing days and was even said to pull pins while performing. The Killers, Blur and The Libertines have also all performed here and the pub is also to this day still used as a live music venue.

At the intersection ahead on Parkway, keep straight ahead passing North Bridge House school on your right. Keep straight at the next intersection too and walk straight with the park on your right towards the White Houses ahead. Follow Gloucester Gate Bridge, then Gloucester Gate and cross Outer Circle to head into Regent's Park.

Look back as you enter the park at the large properties on Gloucester Gate (10), which you just passed and line Regent's Park.

In the Middle Ages, this area was owned by Barking Abbey. However, Henry VIII seized the land in the 16th century and the land is now owned by the Crown Estate.

Until 1649, the land was used as a hunting ground and was known as Marylebone Park. After that the land was leased out for farming activities to individual tenants.

10

In 1811, when the leases expired, the Prince Regent (mentioned earlier in relation to Regent's Canal) had John Nash masterplan the area to include a palace for himself, lodges for his entourage and grand terraced houses around the park. When construction came in 1818, the palace and lodges were dropped but the terraced houses around the park were kept – these are the white ucco building you see today. Regent's Park was opened to the public (on selected days only) in 1835.

he eleven houses on Gloucester Gate, by the park entrance, were designed by Nash and built y Richard Mott in 1827. The buildings are a mixture of commercial units and private residences today. As of January 2018, two of the properties are on the market: one spans two floors nd has four bedrooms and is priced at £4.95 million; the other is laid out over six floors and lso has four bedrooms, plus a mews house at the rear and is priced at £7.5 million. All properties are on the Crown Estate and, therefore, are on a lease for a set number of years.

Once inside Regent's Park, there are two paths – one straight ahead and another to the left take the one to the left, passing a playground on your right. Continue until you reach the nd of this pathway about 300 m later.

To the right, behind the trees, is a red-roofed building with chimneys. This is part of London Zoo (11), the world's oldest scientific zoo dating from 1828. At the annual count, in 2017, the oo had over 20,000 animals.

urn left onto Broad Walk (pathway) and take a look at the fountain.

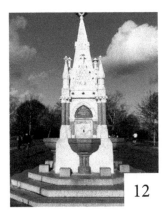

he Ready Money Drinking Fountain (12) is named after a wealthy businessman from Bombay, India called Sir Cowsjee Jehangir, who had the nickname "Ready Money". He was a Parsi (a member of the Zoroastrianism religion) – the British government had offered members of this religion protection from the 17th century onwards during their occupation of parts of the country. "Ready Money" donated the marble and granite sculpture to Regent's Park in 1869 as an expression of gratitude for the protection his religion was offered.

Continue south down Broad Walk past the Drinking Fountain for a further 500 m straight ahead until you reach Chester Road, where cars run along. Be aware that bikes run along the pathway on Broad Walk at considerable speed. By the road is a small café building, with paid toilets behind it.

12

Turn right at the red-pebbled Chester Road and shortly you reach a set of gates on Inner Circle. Go through these and take the pathway immediately to the left to Queen Mary's Rose Gardens (13).

These gardens were the last part of Regent's Park to be made public, having only been created between 1932-1934. The garden is named after Queen Mary, the wife of King George V who reigned from 1910 to 1936. The gardens were re-landscaped in the 1990s by architects Colvin and Moggridge.

There are over 12,000 roses in display in the gardens with over 85 varieties on display, including a unique Royal Parks rose. There is also a begonia garden with 9,000 flowers. This is a great place to sit on a bench for a break and take in the sights and smells of the gardens. If you are walking this route in June count yourself lucky as the flowers are at their peak bloom during this month.

Follow the pathway through the gardens, soon passing a lake to your right hand side. This is the Japanese Garden (14).

The Japanese Garden has a lovely waterfall, an eagle statue presented to the park in the 1970s, plenty of benches and a

14

bow bridge to explore, and actually predates the creation of the Rose Garden you just walked through. It was originally part of the Royal Botanical Society garden which has been based in the park since the 1850s.

Once on the other side of the garden, go through the black and gold gates on your left.

You also have the option of continuing to explore the park before you resume the tour from here – if you turn right, there is a statue of the sea god Triton at the end of the long pathway, as well as the Open Air Theatre. There is also a café with free toilets if you go straight ahead here. The easiest way to find all of these is to use the map by the gates.

We can't possibly cover everything in the park on this tour as the park spans 166 hectares (410 acres), making it the biggest single Royal Park in central London.

Once at the black and gold gates, cross the Inner Circle road and walk down York Bridge – at this point this is just a road, with the bridge further along. Be on the right-hand pavement.

The collection of red buildings to your right as you go along York Bridge is Regents University London (15). It is one of only five fully private universities in the UK.

In contrast to all other universities, such as Oxford or Cambridge Universities, the government does not regulate tuition fees or partially fund Regents University.

In the UK, the government does not own any of the country's universities, nor are its staff civil servants, but most are regulated by it.

15

Regents University is made up of only 15 per cent British students, and mainly educates international students, of which there are about 3600. Alumni include British-American comedian Ruby Wax, Muhammad V of Kelantan (King of Malaysia) and Swedish owner and CEO of H&M, Karl-Johan Persson. Fees are approximately £16,000 per year versus £9,250 at government-regulated universities.

Follow York Bridge. Soon you will cross the bridge itself over Regent Park's boating lake to your right.

Cross the Outer Circle and continue along York Gate towards the church ahead. You will pass more master-planned terraced houses on York Terrace (16), jointly designed by John Nash and Decimus Burton.

Soon, you reach the busy Marylebone Road with St. Marylebone Church (17) opposite – do not cross the road and stay on the pavement on the Regent's Park side.

St. Marylebone Church ahead gives the area you are now in its name – Marylebone. This is the first church on this site having been built in 1813-17, though other St. Marylebone churches have existed in the local area since the 13th century. The name Marylebone comes from the original St. Mary's church being located near a "bourne" or river called Tyburn, eventually corrupting over the years and leading to the current name.

The current building was designed by Thomas Hardwick. The church underwent further alternations in the mid-19th century and restoration following a bomb exploding nearby during The Blitz.

Turn right along Marylebone Road and soon you will come to Madame Tussauds (18).

This famous waxwork museum was the first "Madame Tussauds" location in the world. Marie Tussaud, born in 1761, had a unique job making wax masks before public executions in France.

Just after the French Revolution, Tussaud brought her collection of masks to England in an exhibition. The attraction moved to its current home in 1884.

Today, Madame Tussauds is where you can find true-to-life wax representations of famous figures throughout history – real and imaginary. Inside, there is everyone from David Beckham to Lady Gaga, and The Queen to Albert Einstein. There is also an optional scare zone called the Chamber of Horrors and a ride through the sights of London.

18

Continue ahead along Marylebone Road past Madame Tussauds. Instead of walking along the pavement by the main road, take the pavement alongside the large white building – there are commonly tour buses parked here.

As you reach the entrance to Baker Street station, look out for the statue of the street's most famous detective, Sherlock Holmes (19). The bronze statue was unveiled in 1999 and was designed by John Doubleday.

Baker Street tube station behind you is one of the original stations of the Metropolitan Railway, which was the world's first underground railway, opened in 1863. Inside the station on some platforms and corridors, you will find tiles with Sherlock's portrait on them.

19

Continue past Baker Street Station's entrance and you shortly reach Baker Street. Turn right past another station entrance and about 100 m further on the other side of the road look out for a building with flower pots overflowing out of the windows and Juliette balconies. This is the Sherlock Holmes Museum (20).

The museum is at 221b Baker Street, one of the most famous addresses in the world, and home of the fictional character Sherlock Holmes. You can now explore this Victorian house and move from Sherlock's room to Dr. Watson's and keep an eye out for all the items dotted around, which reference scenes from the books. The museum is very popular, and has limited space as it is in a converted Georgian house, so there is often a queue – an inside visit takes about 20 minutes.

Curiously, if you look at the door numbers, this building shouldn't be number 221 as it lies between 237 and 241 Baker Street. Number 221 should be the tall building on the street, with the tower, called Abbey House a few doors to the left of the museum – historically Abbey House *was* number 221.

In fact, when Abbey National (a bank) moved its headquarters into the new building in 1932, they found that they

20

were receiving letters addressed to Sherlock Holmes. The number of these letters from around the world was so great that the bank employed a member of staff to deal with them. Despite appeals from the Sherlock Holmes Museum to have letters sent to number 221 addressed to Sherlock Holmes delivered to the museum instead, Abbey National Refused.

Since the bank vacated the premises in 2002, the museum has an agreement put in place with Royal Mail to get the letters delivered to the museum instead. To avoid confusion today, Abbey House now has letters displaying the number 219 on its front.

The tour ends here. Retrace your steps back to Baker Street station for the Underground.

Parting Words

You've reach the end of "Amazing London Walks".

Thank you so much for reading and I hope you enjoyed following these walks. You may be interested in my travel guide for London called "The Independent Guide to London 2018", available at Amazon and other book retailers in both print and digital formats - I cover places to stay, things to do, where to eat, the transport system and so much more.

If you have any questions about the walks, want to let me know how you got on, or want to suggest improvements or changes, please get in touch using the form at the bottom of our website at independentguidebooks.com.

If your reading device isn't displaying the maps clearly enough, please visit http://bit.ly/amaz-ingwalks to download high-quality versions of the maps in this guide. On the website, you can right-click the maps and print these out if you wish. If you cannot get these to work, do get in touch via the first link on this page and I will try to help.

Please do leave this book a review at the website you bought it from – these make a huge difference to an independently published author like myself who doesn't have the marketing power that many others do.

Finally, if you would like a private tour of London's neighbourhoods, whether one of those featured in the book or a custom day, visit www.plondontours.com and let's make it happen or contact me through the form at independentguidebooks.com.

Happy travels!

- G. Costa

Photo Credits:
Inside: Lanesborough hotel - Elliott Brown; Royal Artilley Memorial - Amanda Slater; Wellington Arch - Leigh Ann; St. James's Palace, Bloomberg HQ and 55 Broadway- David Holt; Clarence/Lancaster House - Eurovizion; Queen's Guards - atl10trader; Buckingham Palace - Bastique; Canada Gates - Ian Dick; Spencer House and Banqueting House - Steve Cadman; Westminster Abbey - Giusseppe Milo; The Sanctuary - Cary Bass-Deschenes; Buxton Memorial - Paul Wilkinson; Emmeline Pankhurst statue - lutefisk73; Houses of Parliament - Aaron Bradley; Jewel Tower - Cristian Bortes; Oliver Cromwell statue - David Mallett; Government Offices Great George Street - Carlos Delgado; Downing Street - Garry Knight; Horse Guards Parade - Dan Davison; Eleanor Cross - David Short; St Martin's - Mike Procario; Shakespeare's Globe - Neil Willsey; Walkie Talkie - Ungry Young Man; City Hall - Bill Smith; Mansion house - Andrew Milligan Sumo;

Big Ben (cover) - Adam Asap; St Paul's (cover) - loco steve; Tower Bridge (cover) - Santosh Puthran; Eric Titcombe (cover) - Victoria Memorial; Royal Albert Hall (cover) - David Holt; Neal's Yard (cover) - Mikel Ortega; Marble Arch - Paul Hudson, Walkie Talkie Building - Gary Ullah.

All other photos were taken by the author.

Maps provided by OpenStreetMap.

CPSIA information can be obtained
at www.ICGtesting.com
Printed in the USA
BVHW06s0045260618
519964BV00018B/1041/P

9 781986 158268